THE CONCEPT OF ECONOMIC AND POLITICAL DOCTRINE

THE CONCEPT OF ECONOMIC AND POLITICAL DOCTRINE

FRANCO BURGERSDIJK

TRANSLATED BY CAELANUS UMBRA

Edited by
Cody Justice

SACRA PRESS

SACRA AD GLORIAM DEI

Published by Sacra Press.

Franco Burgersdijk, *The Concept of Economic and Political Doctrine*.
Translated by Caelanus Umbra.
Human translated, AI-assisted.
Preface by Stephen Wolfe.
Edited & designed by Cody Justice.
© 2025 by Sacra Press

This is a non-critical, popular edition of this work.

Sacra Press
www.sacrapress.com
contact@sacrapress.com or sacrapress@gmail.com

First edition.
Printed in the United States of America.

Go to www.sacrapress.com
for more reformed, right-wing, & classic books, music, and art,
to become a subscriber, to commission a work, and more.

Godspeed and goodwar.

CONTENTS

The Concept of Economic Doctrine

The Concept of Political Doctrine

PREFACE

BY STEPHEN WOLFE

F RANCO BURGERSDIJK (1590-1635), a name lost in time, was highly influential throughout Europe in the 17th century, mainly for his work on Aristotelian logic. Today, only a select few scholars know of Burgersdijk, and for them his relevance lies only in the history of philosophy. His logic text, *Institutionum Logicarum*, was used widely in European universities until it was eclipsed by the work and criticism of eminent figures in philosophy such as Rene Descartes, John Locke, and G. W. Leibniz.

But whatever one might think of Burgersdijk's brand of logic (the basic form of which is still taught in classical schools throughout the United States), he was a learned man and committed to systematic thinking, orderly presentation, and strict method. Like many Reformed Protestants of his day, he was an Aristotelian not only in his logic but also in natural philosophy and in the disciplines of practical philosophy (ethics, home economy, and politics).

In his *The Concept of Economic and Political Doctrine*, which is now republished for the first time in centuries, he does not cite Aristotle. Indeed, he offers no citations or quotations at all, not even Scripture. It is clear, however, that the ideas contained herein reflect the positive reception of classical sources among Europeans in the late 16th and early 17th centuries. As is evident from the opening page, this work completes his summarizing project in practical philosophy, which begins with ethics (moral philosophy pertaining to the individual) and then proceeds to oeconomica (or home-management) and then to civil politics. One finds this threefold division of practical philosophy in the works of fellow Reformed thinkers, such as Bartholomew Keckermann, Johann Alsted, and many others. The progression from ethics, to households, to politics reflects the classical position that individual public interest is mediated through the household, such that the head of household is the formal and principal public actor—who represents his family's interest and aligns the household with the public good.

Economic life before industrial capitalism was centered on productive households, and so "economics" concerned home management and the material relations between households. Despite developments in the now-distinct field of (political) economics, Burgersdijk's discussion of economics remains relevant, especially for those today who seek to recover productive households and who believe (as I do) that the household, not the individual, is the basic unit of civil society. Civil society is fundamentally composed of families, and political institutions should reflect that.

The second and larger part of this book is on the art of politics, or its practice. Its principal audience are students who expect to be civil rulers in some capacity. The modern reader has likely taken civics or government or perhaps "political science" courses—the stated purpose of which was to make you a good "citizen." But Burgersdijk's interest, reflecting a less democratic time, was to instruct men in the art of civil governance in an era with fewer constitutional constraints. Today, we Christians talk about how to "engage" our neighbors, to be "winsome," and to "contend" in a liberal public square. Burgersdijk's object was the instruction of *public men* in the art of rule for public virtue and piety. Our "Christian politics" today is reduced to "witness" in the public square or the persuasion of fellow citizens by means of "faithful presence." But for our spiritual forefathers, the end of politics was public righteousness by means of God-ordained civil power.

In Burgersdijk's day (like our own), there was no shortage of books on politics and economics, some quite long and made tedious with historical examples and political theory. But Burgersdijk's work on home economy and politics gets to the essence of things—to the marrow of economic and political doctrine. It is suitable for instruction, memorization, and discussion. For us, in addition to these purposes, it exposes us to an early modern mind, in part by sheer contrast. Our experiences in the 20th century and the subsequent dominance of modern liberalism in mind and heart has led us to cast labels of "totalitarianism," "authoritarianism," and "statism" across millennia of political thought. We should not, to be sure, cast aside recent political experience, nor dismiss constitutional developments. But, at the very least, this little book reminds us that our forefathers unreservedly affirmed that civil power is ordained of God for civil good and that Christians ought to wield it for the good and righteousness of one's people.

EPISTLE TO THE READER

TO THE KIND READER, SALUTATIONS.

I have undertaken the task, Kind Reader, to publish the works of the most illustrious man, formerly a worthy professor of our academy, Franco Burgersdijk, metaphysically extracted from the author's own manuscript. For these magnificent meditations have been received with such applause that it has compelled me to pass them on: they are worthy of attention. Moreover, many notable individuals have urged me, with persistent requests, to publish further works by this same great man, which have not yet appeared, showcasing his genius and diligence. In response to their honorable request, and in order to satisfy them, I have pursued this with utmost diligence, engaging in consultation with learned individuals. Here now is the Economic and Political Doctrine, entirely as the author himself has arranged in his interspersed writings. Thus, I ought to express gratitude, as this work serves as a complement to the remaining philosophical meditations of our great Burgersdijk.

There is nothing more to mention on this matter. I easily recognize the dignity and utility of those disciplines, which rightly constitute the reason for governing and guiding the affairs of states and communities. This care pertains to the public schools' pulpits. Therefore, my sole study is to serve you in this endeavor. I will continue to do so in the future, if I learn that it has been pleasing to you. In the meantime, may you benefit from this labor through my efforts.

THE CONCEPT OF
ECONOMIC DOCTRINE

1:

On the Nature of Economy

I. Elsewhere, we have proposed Ethics, or the common part of Practical Philosophy, which contains general precepts of life that must be followed by all people, in any condition or state of life. Here, we will explain the special part, which adds to those general precepts specific instructions for the proper management of a family or household and of the Republic or state. For this part prescribes to each member of the family or citizen what is fitting to their condition and useful for preserving domestic and civil society.

II. This part is divided into Economy and Politics.

III. The term "Economy" is Greek, composed of two words, one meaning house or family, the other meaning to distribute or manage. In Latin, it may be expressed as the discipline or science of managing or governing a family.

IV. "Politics" derives from the Greek word polis, which signifies city or Republic. Thus, according to its etymology, Politics is nothing other than the doctrine of properly establishing and governing the Republic.

V. Therefore, the object of Economy is the house or family; the object of Politics is the city or Republic.

VI. The family is a society of people subject to the authority of the head of the household, just as the Republic is a society of several families living under the same magistrate and laws.

VII. The Republic is composed of families, as parts make up a whole, just as a family is composed of individual persons.

VIII. It follows, then, that domestic society is naturally prior to political society; hence, Economy should be taught before Politics. For just as a household is simpler than a city, and domestic society is more necessary than civil society, so too, economic precepts precede political ones.

IX. For as Ethics relates to Politics and Economy, so Economy relates to Politics. Ethics alone cannot make a person happy without the precepts of Politics and Economy, although it describes and promises happiness. Similarly, Economy cannot achieve the happiness proposed for families outside of Political Society. Indeed, a single family can scarcely, if at all, have everything necessary for living well and happily.

X. Economy indeed has a certain good, as its proposed end, but this end is nothing more than a means to a further and more perfect end, which is the happiness of the Republic. For a family cannot be happy by itself, but only within a well-established Republic.

XI. The parts of Economy are twofold: the first concerns the persons who make up the family, and the second concerns the things necessary for the establishment and preservation of domestic society.

2:

On the Head of the Household

I. The head of the household is the head of the family, and by his command and judgment, all the members of the family are united and governed. Therefore, much more is required from the head of the household than from the other members of the household.

II. First, it is required that the head of the household be a good man and diligently commend virtue to his household. For virtue gives value and respect to all other things necessary in a family.

III. Secondly, he should ensure that all members of the household are obedient and well-behaved, yet this obedience should not stem from fear but from benevolence and love. For fear is not a long-lasting teacher of duty.

IV. Thirdly, he must prescribe to each member of the household what must be done, not only instructing them but also teaching them how each task should be performed and directing them while they work; at least he should be present to encourage them and contribute his own effort to further the work. However, he should remember not to involve himself in trivial matters.

V. Fourthly, it is required that he punish those who do not perform their duty and reward those who are diligent and good.

VI. Fifthly, he must provide all things necessary for the use of his household members and prudently distribute these according to the status and position each person holds in the family.

VII. Sixthly, he should be diligent, industrious, and patient in acquiring resources necessary for the happiness of the family, and he should use these resources not wastefully but liberally.

VIII. Seventhly, he should record all transactions so that the accounts of income and expenses are always clear to him. To facilitate this, records of income and expenses should be kept on opposing pages, with the reasons for each, especially for expenses, noted.

IX. Eighthly and lastly, it is necessary that the head of the household direct the management of his household toward the public good. For he must never benefit his family in such a way that it is detrimental to the Republic.

X. From these points, it follows that a good and prudent head of the household should be not only a good citizen but also highly suited to govern the Republic.

3:

On Conjugal Society

I. In a complete family, there are three types of society: first, between husband and wife; second, between parents and children; and third, between master and servants.

II. Marriage is a natural society of man and woman in the human race, instituted for the procreation of children, mutual assistance, and the legitimate restraint of wandering lust.

III. All human society is indeed natural (for man is by nature a highly sociable animal, and therefore he is given speech; he could not live happily if he excluded himself from society), but the most natural of all societies is the conjugal society. It arises from the most natural desire of perpetuating one's kind and guarding against extinction. Since living beings, due to the frailty of matter, cannot endure forever, nature has ordained that they should renew themselves by perpetual succession. For this reason, the distinction of sex was established by nature.

IV. Moreover, marriage is ordained by nature not only for the perpetuation of the human race but also for happiness. For with the mutual help of spouses, common labor is more easily borne. And the procreation of children offers the greatest assistance to the elderly and infirm parents. Finally, the distinction of sexes is also useful for various economic functions, some of which are more suitable for men, and others for women. For example, as women tend to love more tenderly, they excel in nurturing, while men, loving with greater judgment, are better at providing instruction.

V. Although marriage is natural, the mode of marriage should be circumscribed by specific laws drawn from a more refined culture, so that it is not a promiscuous union like that of animals.

VI. The laws of marriage are either common to both sexes or particular to each. The common laws are derived from many principles.

VII. First, marriage should only be contracted between two people, a male and a female, who are not closely related by blood or kinship. Thus, both polygamy and the union of parents and children, or of brothers and sisters, should be avoided.

VIII. Second, marriage should be chaste and inviolable. Each spouse should not only avoid adultery (as nothing is more intolerable to spouses) but also any just suspicion of adultery. The faithfulness between spouses should be so great that they would only contemplate divorce in the case of the most heinous offenses, choosing rather to die than to separate from each other.

IX. Third, marriage should be harmonious and peaceful. To establish harmony, it is very useful and almost necessary, first, that all things be shared between the spouses; second, that they be equal in age, status, and wealth; third, that the husband love his wife's relatives as his own, and vice versa.

X. The particular laws are either to be observed by the husband or by the wife. For the husband, the primary concerns are the choice of a wife and her governance. In choosing a wife, greater consideration should be given to her piety and virtue than to her beauty or dowry.

XI. In governing his wife, the husband should remember that he is indeed the head of the family, but he should also consider his wife as his partner. Thus, the domestic government resembles political governance, where the husband is like the supreme magistrate and the wife like a subordinate magistrate. Therefore, he should keep his wife in line through prudent persuasion and gentle admonition rather than harsh words or fits of anger.

XII. The wife, on the other hand, should respect her husband as her superior and wiser, conforming herself to his will and character as far as piety and virtue allow. Thus, she should value her husband's virtues highly, regarding them as a law for herself, and express this openly with modesty of affections and grace of words.

4:

On Parental Society

I. From conjugal society arises parental society as a kind of fruit, which serves as a bond obliging parents to mutual love, and therefore, it deserves the greatest care after conjugal society.

II. Parental society consists in the relationship between parents and children, and therefore the duties of parents towards their children and of children towards their parents are to be considered.

III. Parents, by natural instinct, have benevolence towards their children and willingly endure the burdens of their duties out of self-love, which extends beyond themselves to their children, who participate in their parents' substance and efforts.

IV. The general duties of parents are threefold: to properly procreate children, to raise them, and to guide them to a respectable way of life.

V. In the generation of children, parents should ensure, as much as lies within their power, that they produce healthy and strong children. This will be achieved if each parent provides mature and healthy seed, and the mother maintains a suitable diet during pregnancy.

VI. The upbringing of children includes their nourishment, instruction, and discipline, and it varies according to the different stages of age. Nourishment includes not only food but also clothing and other necessities for a healthy diet.

VII. In general, nourishment should be appropriate to the age and constitution of the child's body, contributing to their health and strength, which leads to specific rules.

VIII. First, if possible, infants should be nourished with their mother's milk; if not, a nurse who is chaste, well-mannered, healthy, and recently given birth (and not currently pregnant) should be chosen to prevent the child from acquiring diseases of mind and body.

IX. Second, as the infant grows, if the mother's milk is insufficient, other milk or light broths and easily digestible foods should be introduced, avoiding solid and rich foods, as well as anything containing excess qualities, such as wine and spices.

X. Third, after weaning, children should gradually be introduced to solid food, to build strength and resilience. They should be fed frequently and in moderation rather than excessively at once to avoid the gluttony and associated diseases that often afflict growing children.

XI. Fourth, while the child's limbs are still tender and malleable, they should be properly supported to prevent deformities or to correct any existing ones.

XII. Fifth, children should be gradually accustomed to endure the elements to strengthen them, without exposing them to the harmful effects of severe weather in their early years.

XIII. The education of children should be liberal and suitable to their age and future way of life. This includes private and public instruction that addresses both mind and body.

XIV. Both parents and public instructors should focus on instructing children not only in precepts but also in moral integrity, so that they do not harm their reputation more by poor conduct than they benefit from the teachings.

XV. The mind should first be trained in true piety and virtue, followed by skills that will be useful in the future. Children should learn to read and write, acquire languages that are essential, study disciplines that prepare them for their chosen way of life, and most importantly, be taught the trade they will practice.

XVI. Physical exercises should also be suitable, promoting growth and strength without harming the mind. The exercise should be honorable and liberal, not too strenuous or too slow, and serve as a preliminary for tasks to be performed in adulthood.

XVII. Any education should have breaks and relaxations that allow for some indulgence of the child's will, but care must be taken that these relaxations do not lead to corrupt influences.

XVIII. A more careful and diligent education is suitable for males, while a more lenient but sufficient education is suitable for females, as men's virtues are higher and more challenging, being ruling in nature, while women's virtues are more obedient and easier.

XIX. Discipline for children should be liberal, moderate, and reserved only for parents or those in their place. It should emphasize the dignity of virtues rather than relying on excessive punishment.

XX. The final duty of parents is to guide children to a suitable way of life, preparing them for marriage if they have reached maturity, and providing the necessities for establishing a new household. Once this is accomplished, parents may consider their duty complete.

XXI. The duty of children toward their parents consists in this: 1. They ought to love and revere their parents. 2. They should assist them, and, if necessary, even support them. For neither gratitude for the benefits from parents nor due respect for their dignity can be shown without these things.

5:

On the Servile Society

I. The last society in a perfect household is that of the servant: in which it is necessary to understand what a master and a servant are, then to consider the origin of this society, and finally what the duties of each are within the society.

II. The lord is a person of his own law, from whose direction another depends. The servant, on the other hand, is a person of another's law, who depends on the direction of another.

III. This Society has its origin both from nature, from law, and from contract. From nature indeed it begins; in that some are endowed with a superior mind and fit for command, while their bodies are weak and unfit for labor: others are endowed with a dull mind and inclined to obey; if they are robust in body, and capable of enduring labors, it is useful for those to command, and for these to serve, so that in fact each may prosper in their respective needs.

IV. From law arises servitude, when captives in war or those made captive by disgraceful acts, or by voluntary sale, after they have reached the age of discretion, have lost the right to liberty and are compelled to servile duties, whether public or private; such servitude, however, has almost been abolished among Christians.

V. By contract, a servant is called when a free person subjects himself to the authority of another for a certain reward or compensation, either perpetually or for a specified time.

VI. This servitude almost exclusively prevails among Christians and is one of the most just, because it stands best with the natural liberty of all men.

VII. Those who are called servants and mentioned are analogous to servants or handmaids, and those in charge of a household, for they too are subjected to the authority of magistrates as if they were under them.

VIII. The duties of lords with respect to servants include selection, governance, and management of the servants, which involves consideration of what is due to the servants.

IX. It is particularly fitting to choose boys born and raised in the household as servants, or to care for those born elsewhere to be raised in the home, so that they may more easily and better become accustomed to domestic instruction. However, if this cannot be done, adults should be chosen, but they should be as few as possible and not subject to many vices: the very bold should not be admitted, nor the very timid. For boldness makes them insolent and rebellious; fear makes them cowardly or despairing. Servants should fear their master, but they should also love him.

X. Servants are owed sustenance, protection, work, and discipline. By sustenance is meant food, drink, clothing, and payment.

XI. Food and drink should be generously provided to servants, sufficient for their satisfaction and strength. Wine or delicacies should rarely be granted to them.

XII. Clothing for servants should be for necessity, not for adornment, unless it pertains to the splendor of the masters; even servants should be dressed decorously.

XIII. Wages should be faithfully paid to servants, and this based on a contract. For there is no greater injustice than not paying wages to those who work. And God prescribes the manner of paying wages very carefully, not allowing anyone to lie down without wages being paid to servants.

XIV. Moreover, if servants are ill, they should be cared for humanely, as they are useful to their masters; and if they die, they should be buried honorably.

XV. Servants should be educated, as private and public utility demands. Education should be suited to the character of each; for some are to be prepared for more liberal tasks, others for less liberal ones, either by the masters themselves or by those to whom the masters entrust this matter.

XVI. Furthermore, education should not only include disciplines or arts suitable for servants, but also virtues and moderation; they should be instructed in virtues from a young age: obedience, diligence, loyalty, and silence.

XVII. Work and tasks for servants should be prescribed, so that they are not neglected in idleness and do not become lazy. However, the work of servants should be prescribed according to dimensions and times; and they should be allowed to rest after their labor is complete unless their duties are such that they cannot be prescribed a time.

XVIII. Finally, servants should also be disciplined, lest from impunity contempt follow. The discipline of servants pertains to the masters themselves or to those to whom this duty has been entrusted. And although the discipline of servants should be more severe than that of free persons, it should still adhere to a mode fitting for humanity. For the cruelty of the ancient pagans towards servants is contrary to nature.

XIX. As discipline should correspond to offenses, so should sustenance, rest, labor, wages, and similar things vary according to the different industries and natures of the servants; and also the wages should frequently be increased, so that they serve all the more diligently.

XX. Those who have many servants should distinguish them into different ranks: so that some are inspectors and directors of affairs, others are laborers.

XXI. Since a servant is nothing other than an instrument of the master, it will not be difficult to understand the duties of servants; all of which are arranged so that they obey their masters and diligently and faithfully execute everything that is commanded by those masters (provided it does not conflict with honesty), in which all their actions should regard the comfort and honor of their masters.

6:

On the Imperfect Family

I. And this tripartite society constitutes a perfect family. But if any other society is interposed, such as that which exists between a host and guests who are received, it does not pertain to the constitution of the family.

II. Nevertheless, the head of the family should not scorn hospitality; for this is a virtue and part of liberality.

III. Just as a perfect family consists of a tripartite society, so too is it necessary for a family to have one or more societies desired.

IV. However, it is greatly mutilated in which the head of the family is lacking. From this, great inconveniences arise in the family, creating a sort of anarchy. For it is difficult for a widow to hold authority so as to keep all family members in duty.

V. Nevertheless, this may be somewhat remedied if the son of the family is of age to take on the governance of the family.

VI. The second imperfection of the family is where a widower governs; for here, little consideration can be given to infants or to children who are not yet adults, who have been left by a deceased father or mother, nor to those things which pertain to the internal governance of the household.

VII. The third imperfection is found in a sterile family. For the bonds of marital love are lost, heirs of the household property are absent, and the greatest solace of old age is lacking.

VIII. The fourth imperfection is in that family where, due to extreme poverty, there are servants, where each one is for himself as a servant, or uses a servant for help.

IX. The fifth and greatest imperfection of the family is when the celibates establish a household, and they themselves either perform all domestic duties or rely on the service of servants or handmaids.

7:

On Various Types of Possessions

I. We have spoken of the persons that constitute the household; it remains to discuss those things which are necessary for living simply or comfortably in a domestic society, which are all understood under the name of possessions.

II. And here three things should be considered: First, how many types of possessions there are; second, what are the methods of acquiring possessions; third, what is the manner of using possessions in domestic matters.

III. Possession can be either animate or inanimate. Animate refers to a servant or livestock. And a servant is counted among possessions because he is the most distinguished instrument of the master, by whom the rest of the instruments and all domestic supplies are managed.

IV. Among the livestock that constitute domestic possessions, the first place is held by cattle, such as oxen, and the like. The second includes flocks, such as sheep, goats, and the like. The third includes birds, such as sparrows, chickens, doves, and the like. The fourth includes dogs and cats, or any other animals that are appropriate.

V. Inanimate possession is either natural or artificial. Among natural possessions, the first includes land, fields, vineyards, gardens, ponds, lakes, forests, mines, and the like. The second includes fruits produced from these, such as grains, legumes, plums, apples, fish, wood, hay, straw, and the like.

VI. Among artificial possessions, the first place is held by the house, which, if it is to be inhabited, must be healthy, pleasant, and convenient for the remaining resources and domestic functions. The second place is held by various types of supplies, which either serve necessity, or comfort, or for the adornment of things, such as clothing, beds, paintings, and the like. The third place includes instruments for both culinary and manual labor. The fourth includes weapons, medicines, and books. The fifth includes money.

8:

On Acquiring Possessions

I. It is not only permissible but also necessary to increase domestic possessions and household wealth, provided that it is done by honest means, nor should any head of a family be able to neglect this care.

II. Therefore, the head of the family ought to be knowledgeable about those things which are to be acquired and to know how each should be acquired; and he should also be laborious and frugal; and finally, just, so that by the benefit of this virtue, no one may be harmed, and he himself may not indulge in any shameful acts.

III. There are three legitimate ways of acquiring possessions: one is natural, the second artificial, and the third is a mixture of both.

IV. Natural acquisition is that which nature, in urgent necessity, teaches us to acquire for sustenance. This can be through agriculture, pastoralism, hunting, mining, forestry, or finally through barter.

V. Agriculture is a way of acquiring from the land and the fruits that grow on it. This is the most natural, just, and useful method: for it cultivates the strength of the body and prepares it for martial virtue.

VI. Pastoralism is the method of acquiring sustenance through the care and pasture of domesticated animals.

VII. Hunting is the method of acquiring sustenance through the capture of wild animals. It can be either fowling, fishing, or hunting in the strict sense, which is concerned with investigating inferior creatures.

VIII. Metalworking or metallurgy is when metals, such as gold, silver, bronze, iron, and similar substances, are extracted for our use. Here, the artisan also produces objects by working with metals, such as crafts and alchemy, which fall under artificial methods.

IX. Forestry acquisition is from the cutting of woods.

X. Barter is when we acquire necessary items for the household; we give to others in exchange for what we need ourselves.

XI. Among all these methods, the first three pertain to food; the following refer to those things that are useful for procuring food. Thus, the first three are somewhat more natural than the latter. Barter seems to stray further from nature. However, since nature has given more to some than is needed, and less to others, and not to all, it seems that it willed that deficiencies should be made up through barter.

XII. Thus, having discussed natural acquisition, we turn to artificial acquisition. Artificial acquisition is that which approaches closer to the will and industriousness of humans than to the providence of nature.

XIII. And this can be either private or public. Private acquisition is that by which something is acquired from private properties. It can be through commerce, money lending, labor, or hospitality.

XIV. Commerce is the method of acquiring through buying and selling. Its instrument and measure is money. It differs from barter, which occurs without money.

XV. Commerce, therefore, has been invented for the convenience of barter. For either the distance between places, the variety of goods, or the necessity often hinders barter; which impediments commerce removes by the benefit of money.

XVI. Therefore, commerce is a legitimate method of acquisition if it is used to supply the deficiencies of nature. But if it is referred to increasing wealth without any ulterior motive, it becomes contrary to nature, as it would progress infinitely. For money is an instrument of barter; in contrast, the instruments of nature are meant to be multiplied to a finite end.

XVII. There are three types of commerce: maritime, freight, and retail. Maritime commerce is that by which goods are transported to distant regions by ship; freight commerce is conducted by animals and vehicles over land; retail commerce is that in which goods are bought and sold in the same location.

XVIII. Some commerce is more liberal, while others are sordid. The more liberal commerce is conducted with great expenditures and deals in goods that do not harm the body. Conversely, sordid commerce deals in goods sold in small quantities, which do harm the body.

XIX. Money lending is that which profits from money. It can be either interest, exchange, or guarantee.

XX. Interest is when something is borrowed for money and the lender receives something in return based on the amount lent. If the money lent does not acquire anything for the borrower, nor is it lent solely to supply the necessities of life, it seems to be contrary to both natural and divine law to demand interest. For money is sterile; therefore, it cannot generate profit. But if money is not used to supply life's necessities but is used for profit, it is quite equitable and in accordance with nature that the portion of profit allowed by public magistrates should go to the lender. This is not only a matter of gratitude but also of justice. For if profit can be derived from leasing a house or estate, why not from money? Certainly, God forbids usury among brothers; others he does not permit. (Deut. 20:19)

XXI. Exchange is a type of money lending that makes profit from the exchange of money or from transactions made at various locations; for this purpose, safe coins were invented to transfer money without risk, deducted from the value of the coin.

XXII. A guarantee is when someone, having received a certain sum of money, promises to cover the loss of goods sent to distant regions, should they perish by shipwreck or be captured by pirates. This type of money lending is called assurance by the French.

XXIII. Labor is when someone offers their service for pay; it can be either skilled or unskilled labor: the former practice mechanical arts, such as carpenters, weavers, and so forth; the latter offer labor without expertise, such as day laborers.

XXIV. Hospitality seeks sustenance from receiving guests.

XXV. And these are the methods of acquiring possessions from private matters. Those who acquire from the public either offer their services for the public good, or in war, such as soldiers, or in peace; and they either serve the Republic, such as counselors, questors, or professors in schools; or they serve the church, such as clerics.

XXVI. There remains a third method of acquisition that is neither natural nor artificial; this includes inheritances, donations, the discovery of treasure; likewise, disputes over uncertain goods based on deposit.

9:

On the Use of Possessions

I. We have discussed acquiring possessions; it remains for us to address the proper management of acquired goods in the administration of the household for daily life.

II. Acquired goods should be used first for necessity, second for enjoyment, and third for adornment.

III. The head of the family should take care not to let expenses exceed revenues.

IV. He should also consider what expenses can be reduced without causing inconvenience to the household.

V. Fifth, he should strive to ensure that, as much as possible, the land and other kinds of possessions are the most fruitful.

VI. Resources should be distributed in such a way that not all can easily perish at once. Above all, merchants should not be entrusted to expend all resources at once on a single type of goods.

VII. The care and administration of the household is to be shared between husband and wife; when the husband is absent, the entire responsibility should fall to the wife. And the household should never be left unattended at any time.

VIII. The master of the servants should oversee them himself; he should rise first and go to bed last. If this cannot be done, the task should be entrusted to a steward.

IX. Food should be prepared correctly so that it is not spoiled, and should be suitably prepared and cooked.

X. The household should be kept clean and tidy, with utensils and clothing well-maintained to avoid attracting dirt. Each tool should be stored in its proper place, and those used less frequently should be set aside separately.

XI. The master should regularly check the supplies and household instruments to see what has gone bad or has been completely lost.

XII. There are two methods of managing a household: The first is when the head of the family sells all his revenues annually and uses the gathered money to purchase what is necessary for life from other sources. The second is when he only sells surplus items, keeping what is necessary for his domestic use.

XIII. The latter method is preferable. The former is suitable only for the poor; wealthier individuals should not follow it unless they carefully deduct their annual income sum.

XIV. All these principles of economy, which we have thus far presented, should be prudently adapted to each individual's condition. For the economy of a king should differ from that of a prince, a count, a baron, a noble, merchants, artisans, magistrates, and subjects. Moreover, the economy in Germany should differ from that in France, Poland, and so forth.

THE CONCEPT OF
POLITICAL DOCTRINE

1:

On the Nature of the Republic

I. Politics is the doctrine (as has been said) of rightly constituting and governing the Republic. For these two are so connected that they cannot be separated. And although a Republic is not always to be established, nevertheless, no one should be deemed to govern a Republic unless he has the ability to establish it.

II. A Republic is a society of many families under the same magistracy, living under the same laws. Moreover, it is a summative power of families and a moderate multitude regulated by reason.

III. From this, it follows that a Republic cannot consist of a single family, no matter how numerous it may be, but at least two, and minimally three, because three persons are necessary for the constitution of a collegium.

IV. Secondly, it follows that a band or gang of robbers is not a Republic, because although it can be formed from several families, it cannot be called a Republic since it is not governed by right reason.

V. Political society, or the political community, has its origin in nature. For man is by nature a political animal, which is evident both from his speech and from his use of it.

VI. However, this inclination of nature has been stimulated by both need and danger. Because one family cannot supply everything necessary for living well and for repelling violence or injury, which is often inflicted by others, several families have joined together and formed a society.

VII. To avoid confusion at these borders, all have submitted themselves to the authority of a few, or even of one, in which they have perceived wisdom and extraordinary courage.

VIII. Therefore, it is false what some political theorists teach, that empires and republics first arose from violence and that the highest power of command emerged from this. For it was not the case that the remaining multitude submitted to the authority of one, because he led them in war, and that he emerged victorious because of his followers; but rather, they united under him so that superior wisdom and strength would prevail.

IX. Political society arose from humble beginnings. Initially, a few families formed a neighborhood. I call these families "gentile," which are bound together by a common origin, connected by blood. Subsequently, even foreign families joined the gentiles, increasing the number of families, leading to the establishment of villages first, and then cities.

X. At first, the political society seemed sufficiently secure to ward off external injuries and was adequately structured to provide all the comforts of life; but later, with the increase of human malice, cities began to be surrounded by walls, trenches, and moats to be safer, not only against external violence but also against the rebellion and malice of natives.

XI. Furthermore, several cities have been reduced to the same Republic by forming alliances, whether by pact or by the law of war, or by force. By pact, several cities contract alliances to live more securely with mutual assistance. By the law of war, when a city has been conquered by arms, it falls under the power of another.

XII. And certainly, it seems expedient for human affairs for a Republic to be constituted from several cities, since each does not have sufficient resources to live well and to transfer across borders.

XIII. The aim of political doctrine is to secure the universal Republic, which consists in ensuring that all live piously and honorably; and then that all, as much as possible, may be supported in what is necessary for living well, and in matters common to them, and the common rights of the city are defended against external force. From these two things, tranquility and harmony among citizens arise, which is the greatest good of the Republic.

XIV. The public happiness of the Republic is achieved through the wisdom of governance and through a prompt and benevolent will to serve. This is required of the magistrates; and this regarding the subjects.

XV. And although it is more esteemed to govern than to be governed, to command than to obey, it is nonetheless true that Machiavelli teaches that subjects must submit simply to the prince, in whose municipalities they are free to dominate at will. Conversely, magistrates exist for the sake of their subjects. For a political society is not formed from many unless it is for the well-being of individuals within that society. For this to happen, magistrates must diligently work, governing prudently.

2:

On Monarchy and
the Natural Gifts of a Monarch

I. Politics or the state of the Republic is either simple or mixed. The simple state is divided into Monarchy, Aristocracy, and Democracy. A Monarchy is a state in which all others are subject to the authority of one.

II. A Monarchy is the simplest and most orderly state; therefore, it is firmly established by its nature. Moreover, this form of governance is easier and achieves its end more readily. However, considering human weakness, it is not always expedient for other forms of government to prefer Monarchy. For often the disposition of subjects cannot endure Monarchy, and also the supreme authority of affairs is precarious when it resides in a single head.

III. In a Monarch or prince, the nature, virtue, and cause of principality must be considered. By nature, I mean the sex, body, homeland, household, age, and fortune. Each of these aspects must be observed.

IV. Therefore, first (starting from sex), the monarchical authority should be entrusted to a male rather than a female. 1. Because the male is the lord of the household and the head of the woman, thus he should also be the head of the Republic. 2. Because the male is fit for commanding, while the female is fit for obeying. 3. Because the female sex is inferior to the male in all the gifts of nature.

V. Nevertheless, women are not to be completely excluded from the Republic and its governance. Because nature often makes women capable; they can be industrious, learned, and prudent through education and experience.

VI. Secondly, the prince must be of a noble stature and beauty; the former contributes greatly to authority, while the latter to benevolence, for almost everyone judges that the external appearance of the body is an indication of the mind.

VII. Thirdly, the prince's authority should preferably be delegated to a native rather than a foreigner. 1. Because a native will love the subjects more and will be loved by them. 2. Because a foreigner will wish to bring about change and to rearrange the Republic according to his own desires, which cannot be done without danger. 3. Because it is disgraceful for anyone to seek an external ruler, as if among those unable to govern.

VIII. However, individual circumstances may sometimes require the necessity of the Republic to call upon a foreign prince, who at that time may restore the Republic with incomparable virtue and power.

IX. Fourthly, the prince must be of noble birth. Because all judge that nobility possesses some virtue and is more inclined to heroic endeavors. 2. For his stem and insignia of nobility, along with the remembrance of great deeds performed by his ancestors, confer reverence and authority upon the prince.

X. Fifthly, the age of the prince should be mature. Thus, a child or a very young adolescent should not be permitted to hold authority. 1. Because he cannot be prudent. 2. Because that age is too flexible. 3. Because he cannot possess authority.

XI. If, however, the principate is handed down through succession, the children of deceased princes are not to be excluded from power; but the magistrates or counselors (as is the parliament in England) should commit the governance of the Republic to one or more nobles, until the prince comes of age, carefully ensuring that guardians do not sell the kingdom for themselves.

XII. Although a vigorous and healthy age is most suitable for the principate, it does not seem equitable that a prince should be deprived of power due to old age if all else in him is in accordance with what is required in a prince, especially if the mind is sound. However, when the mind is corrupted, the prince should be removed from the Republic and another appointed in his place.

XIII. Lastly, in selecting a prince, wealth and power must be considered. For this pertains to the strength of the Republic. And the potentiality of the magistrate should not seem so much to be feared due to insolence, as by the poverty or stupidity that leads to rapacity and tyranny.

3:

On the Education of the Prince

I. Having discussed the nature of the prince or the natural gifts, we now turn to virtue, which can be understood as either mental or moral. Virtue of the mind is nothing other than knowledge or education.

II. Education is required in a prince. 1. Because it leads to prudence and sharpens judgment. For prudence does not easily occur unless the mind is well-instructed and educated.

III. Because it leads to an accurate understanding of the region and the people over whom he must rule.

IV. Because the prince must judge many controversies that cannot be understood without education.

V. Meanwhile, although education is vast and broad, the prince should not need to examine all its parts thoroughly; it is sufficient if he extracts from each enough for practical use.

VI. First, the prince must be imbued with knowledge of languages. Besides his own tongue, the prince should learn Latin and the languages of neighboring or allied nations. Latin should be known because it is universal and known throughout the world. Therefore, he will be able to supplement the deficiencies of many foreign tongues when listening to ambassadors from other princes and responding to them. Not to mention that the Latin language is essential for education, as we have shown.

VII. The languages of neighboring and allied nations should be known to the prince so that he can participate in affairs that are often negotiated with neighboring peoples.

VIII. After languages, Logic must be studied, but Rhetoric should be studied diligently. For eloquence is very necessary in a prince to move and incite the spirits of his subjects. Furthermore, poetry must be dealt with by the prince, not to compose verses himself, but to understand poets, especially the tragic ones.

IX. Next, he should proceed to Theoretical Philosophy, which offers Physics and Mathematics. For Metaphysics is primarily useless. Physics is useful for the prince to understand the nature of the region and people over whom he rules, and for many other things that should not be unknown to him.

X. The prince must learn Mathematical disciplines accurately. Their usefulness is very great, both in peace and in war. In peace, for Architecture and Mechanics; in war, for nearly all preparations. And although the prince may employ the ministry of others for these matters, nevertheless, if he himself understands these disciplines, everything will be conducted more reliably by his ministers.

XI. The prince should study Moral Philosophy sufficiently. For who can govern others if he has not learned the principles of governance, which pertain to Moral Philosophy?

XII. Moral Philosophy must be derived not only from precepts but also from history. For precepts are universal. However, human actions and political prudence, which govern actions, consist of singular instances; of which the judgment of history includes a full narrative. So that there is hardly any part of doctrine so necessary and useful to the prince as an accurate knowledge of histories. Travel also contributes to prudence, but it is not safe for the prince.

XIII. It is not enough to have learned ancient history, that of the Greeks and Romans, but modern history must also be known. In particular, he must be well-acquainted with the history of his own kingdom and that of his ancestors; so that from the counsel and deeds of others, he can gather what should be done for himself.

XIV. Finally, the prince must also deliberate on Jurisprudence and Sacred Theology, the former enabling him to judge disputes among citizens, or at least to appoint just judges in the courts; the latter, so that he may understand the tenets of his religion and discern true religion from false through the word of God, and so legitimately protect and maintain it among his subjects.

4:

On the Moral Virtue Required in a Prince

I. Moral virtue in a prince is required under two names; first, because he himself must be virtuous as a man. For nothing is more suitable for a man than moral virtue. Secondly, because the life of the prince serves as an example for the subjects. There is nothing that has a greater impact on shaping the morals of the subjects, in either direction, than the life of the prince.

II. Moral virtue must be genuine in the prince and not simulated: both because this virtue is the firmest foundation of the Republic, and because what is simulated cannot be lasting.

III. First, prudence is required in the prince. For this is the standard and moderator of the other virtues. By the protection of this virtue, the prince can adapt all virtuous actions to the dignity and excellence of his person. For since the actions of virtues are placed in moderation, which must be adapted to various circumstances, prudence is not necessary in all men, but especially in a prince. This applies not only to ethical virtues but also to political and economic governance.

IV. Prudence is a mean between simplicity or foolishness, and between truthfulness or cunning deceit. If, however, the prince deviates from this mean, it is preferable for him to be shrewd and cunning rather than simple and imprudent, provided that shrewdness is not associated with great malice of spirit.

V. After prudence, we place piety; by this word, both the duty towards God and the love of the subjects are understood, which is a certain piety towards the homeland. 1. Just as impiety and profaneness, or even superstition, in a prince are extremely harmful, so true religion is highly necessary. For he who has established himself as subject to God, to whom all actions must be accounted, will easily temper governance with justice and equity.

VII. Love for the homeland and the subjects will lead the prince to refer all things, not merely to his own interests, but to the well-being of his subjects; so that he will consider himself not only as a prince but also as a shepherd, indeed almost as a parent of his subjects.

VIII. From this it seems to follow that one must be invited to relinquish the principate. 1. Because the love of the subjects cannot be so great in one who rules unwillingly. 2. Because he will administer the Republic more sagely. 3. Because a difficulty arising will reproach the subjects, saying that he was compelled to take up power. Thus, he easily becomes a tyrant.

IX. We assign the third place in a prince to justice, both universal and particular. Universal justice is the virtue of rendering obedience to the laws. Therefore, the prince must also be subject to the laws, or else he cannot be just.

X. However, whether the prince is subject to the laws or not, this matter is often disputed. It seems to me that this question cannot be resolved without distinction. First, in law, there should be a distinction between a mandate and a reward promised for obedience, or a punishment threatened for transgressors. Thus, the law primarily obliges to the performance, and then to punishment if someone violates it. Secondly, there are other fundamental laws, which princes swear to observe before they are admitted to the principate; others are not fundamental laws. With these premises established, I say that the prince is not only obligated to uphold fundamental laws but is also subject to punishment and may lose his principate if he violates them. The prince is also obliged to observe other laws, but is not subject to punishment if he violates them. For punishing is the supreme action of power, yet the prince acknowledges no one among men on earth as superior to himself in this regard. Nevertheless, he must answer to God for the violation of these laws.

XI. Particular justice is divided into distributive and commutative, both of which are necessary in a prince; but especially the former, as it pertains more to the public good.

XII. In the fourth place, we place temperance and chastity, for nothing so easily overthrows empires as intemperance, luxury, and licentiousness. These are also enemies to prudence and cause scandals among subjects.

XIII. To temperance, we add fortitude, diligence, and vigilance: either to avert and decline adverse matters and dangers, or to push them away.

XIV. The most appropriate virtue for a prince is liberality and magnificence, which are most suitable for securing benevolence and authority for himself. Particularly, public liberality is most commendable, such as when tributes are remitted to the people, and it is evident in aid to the poor, afflicted, and exiles, etc. Also, that which is bestowed upon learned men, or excellent artists, or even those who have rendered great service to the Republic through notable deeds.

XV. Meanwhile, the prince must take care not to become prodigal and exhaust the public treasury with immoderate gifts, as this would harm the Republic and incur hatred towards himself. But he should not avoid prodigality so much that he becomes stingy. For this vice is also hateful to subjects and is disgraceful for a prince.

XVI. With magnificence must be joined magnanimity, to safeguard majesty and prevent contempt from arising due to excessive pride or cowardice. Magnanimity relates to seriousness in words, behavior, gestures, clothing, gait, and indeed in all public actions. Although it seems advisable that the prince should not be too frequently present in public, for majesty gains greater reverence from a distance.

XVII. However, since a magnanimous person judges nothing to be greater than honor, if the prince is magnanimous, he should scorn infamy both in life and even after death. Hence, he will be extremely diligent to avoid sins, estimating that the sins of princes are much greater, the greater their splendor and majesty; and although they are very slight, they will seem very grave and will quickly become public.

XVIII. Following this, meekness or clemency is also the greatest ornament of princes. For gentleness befits a prince.

XIX. Moreover, truthfulness and faithfulness are required in a prince, which should be maintained not only towards subjects, allies, and confederates but also towards foreigners and even enemies. For if a prince violates a given pledge, no one will have faith in him, no one will admit his envoys, and no one will wish to enter into any treaty or pact with him.

XX. If the prince loves the truth, he will shun flatterers, for they, as enemies of the truth, are most pernicious to princes.

XXI. The prince must also be gracious, that is, he should readily admit subjects to conversation, listen patiently, respond kindly, and satisfy their petitions, especially if they do not fear treachery. In this way, the opportunity for flatterers to seek gain from those who come to the prince and to obtain what subjects request from him will be curtailed.

XXII. Finally, the prince may concede to urbanity, but in moderation, and at a time when he is free from public cares. Nor should the prince indulge in jesting himself, but should listen to the festive, witty, and honorable jokes of others, while rejecting the rest. Thus, it seems hardly advisable for a prince to amuse himself with buffoons or foolish people. For those whom industry has not favored should not be welcomed.

XXIII. The prince may also amuse himself with music; however, he should neither sing nor play instruments. Games that exercise the body, such as hunting, ball games, etc., are fitting for princes, provided they are free from danger. For they are like preparatory exercises for military matters.

5:

On the Causes of the Principate, or the Ways of Attaining the Principate

I. The way in which a prince is elevated to the principate consists of two parts: by right and by inauguration.

II. The right to the principate is acquired in six principal ways: by succession, election, war, marriage, testament, and chance. Among these, however, the most common and ordinary means of acquiring the right to the principate are succession and election.

III. Although both methods have their advantages and disadvantages, succession seems to suit absolute monarchy more than election. For, first, since a person is elected by the people, he can hardly obtain absolute power and full majesty, since the people generally have the power to enact laws to which the prince must bind himself by oath. Moreover, an interregnum has very serious disadvantages, which succession does not have, since the death of a prince is seldom regarded where one successor immediately follows another. And although it may seem better to be elected than to be born into it, we often see the contrary happen, either due to undue recommendations or factions among equals, or opposing votes, so that princes who are elected are not better than those who succeed. When one knows that by the right of succession he is owed the principate, he usually relies on his own merit to establish his inherited rule.

IV. If a prince has several children, the firstborn from a legitimate marriage should be preferred over his brothers, rather than the kingdom being divided. However, he who succeeds in the principate must assign to his remaining brothers only a portion of the revenues, sufficient for them to live with dignity.

V. The daughters of a prince should either not be elevated to the principate, or if it has already been accepted, they should not be preferred over their brothers, not even if they are older in age.

VI. If one of two sons of a prince is born before the father has attained the principate, and the other after, the firstborn should still be preferred. Indeed, even grandsons from the firstborn should be preferred over their own sons.

VII. It is advisable that the prince designate his successor and declare a vicar for the kingdom, so that upon the prince's death, the same person may succeed him at that very hour, thus avoiding the troubles of an interregnum, which are nothing but perilous.

VIII. As we have said, election is less fitting for absolute monarchy due to the conditions and laws that may prescribe the election of the prince. However, if the prince's family is entirely extinct, so that no one from his line can succeed, it is very useful then for the prince to be designated by votes, which is indeed ordinary in many kingdoms.

IX. Election should occur in public assemblies of the kingdom, through free and uncorrupted votes, so that the person most suited to the principate may be designated from the multitude of votes.

X. The principate is acquired by marital right when the prince marries a woman who is also a princess, and she transmits the principate to her descendants.

XI. Testamentary acquisition occurs when the prince, having designated legitimate heirs, appoints someone of his choosing as his successor in a testament. Succession by covenant can also be recalled: for example, when two princes form a mutual covenant that if one family becomes completely extinct, the descendants of the other should succeed to the principate, such as the pact between the houses of Saxony and Hesse.

XII. If a prince is to be elected, and neither reason nor consensus can be applied, either because the heirs to the kingdom are equal, or because the offense of another who is overlooked is to be feared, this should be avoided; but it must be done in a way that cannot be susceptible to fraud.

XIII. The last mode of acquiring the principate is by arms, or by war. Such a monarchy is harsher and binds the subjects more closely than that which is acquired by ordinary means.

XIV. This can occur in two ways: first, when a prince is driven from power by a just war; second, when barbarous peoples are subjugated who were subject to no prior authority.

XV. Barbarous peoples should not be subjugated out of a desire for domination, as was done by Alexander the Great, but rather to bring men, living almost like beasts, to humanity, honor, and piety.

XVI. And these are the ways by which a prince acquires the principate: it must be through inauguration, or as one is placed into possession, and confirmed by the consent of the people.

XVII. This inauguration consists of certain steps. For, first, the prince is publicly proclaimed; then the insignia of the kingdom are handed over, including the crown, scepter, purple robe, etc. Thirdly, he is led to the temple, where, after the sacred rites are completed and the divine name is invoked, he is initiated with solemn ceremonies, and thus is established in the possession of the principate, with the public acclaim and congratulation of the people approving of the prince's inauguration.

XVIII. Through these acts, the prince acquires the right of majesty, that is, the highest authority over citizens and subjects, and the power to legislate and perpetuate.

XIX. To the right of majesty particularly pertains: 1. To declare war and conclude peace. 2. To enact laws and establish rights. 3. To appoint magistrates. 4. Not to admit challenges. 5. To liberate those sentenced through judicial judgments. 6. To demand loyalty and obedience. 7. To mint currency.

6:

On the Governance of the Prince in General and on Laws

I. Thus far, we have discussed the Person of the Prince and the causes or means of attaining the principate. Now, we shall discuss Governance, or the care of the prince regarding his administration.

II. The care of the prince must be directed towards being a public person, so that he directs all his counsel and actions toward the common good.

III. To achieve this more easily, he should understand the disposition of his subjects. Since he cannot know each individual, he should judge from the general population based on the majority.

IV. Because the people are credulous, fickle, variable, inconsistent, hasty, and vehement, it is primarily the prince's duty to contain them within the limits of obedience.

V. To this end, it is necessary that the prince act personally in all matters, or at least ensure that his subjects are persuaded to see everything with his own eyes rather than through others'.

VI. Moreover, it should not be sufficient for the prince that the Republic benefits him as long as he lives; he should also ensure that it flourishes after his death. Therefore, he must maturely arrange all matters in his testament and appoint executors of that testament. The testament should not be made public. If uncertain, he should name a successor in his testament and ensure that the matter is under his authority. If a successor is certain, he should inform the prince of everything that will most pertain to the safety of the kingdom. If he cannot name a successor within his power, he should commend someone to the nobles whom he deems most suitable for the administration of the kingdom.

VII. The prince should also provide for his wife and children who do not succeed him, assigning them only as much as is sufficient for them to live with dignity. He should also establish certain rewards for faithful ministers, encouraging them to remain loyal to the Republic, the successor, and also to his wife and other children.

VIII. Since the doctrine on the governance of the prince is broad, we will establish certain headings for the sake of order, to which all the duties of the prince will refer. First, we will discuss Laws, or the care of the prince regarding laws. 2. The Prince's Ministers. 3. The nature and education of subjects. 4. The ranks and commonality of citizens. 5. The judicial process and census. 6. The sustenance and health to be maintained, and concerning burial and other matters pertaining to the happiness of citizens. 7. The public revenues. 8. The care of defending, augmenting, and adorning the Republic. 9. The Prince's Court. 10. Regarding foreigners. 11. Concerning ambassadors. 12. On treaties. 13. Regarding war. 14. On the causes of changes and the vices of the principate.

IX. A law (as I begin) is a rule concerning those things that are to be done or omitted, so that the Republic may be governed happily.

X. A law is either divine or human. Human law can be the law of nature, the law of nations, or political or economic law.

XI. Political law (to say nothing of the others) pertains to the Republic. It can be either a norm for undertaking or for governing the principate. Laws for undertaking the principate are called fundamental laws and the oaths of the kingdom.

XII. The laws for governing the principate are those according to which the prince commands the subjects, and the subjects obey the prince. For although the prince may be free from the laws, nevertheless, the laws must serve as a standard for the prince according to which he governs his subjects.

XIII. The law considers sanction, execution, interpretation, and abrogation. All these matters pertain to the prince by right; however, it is expected that wise and just men be consulted by him for advice, whose work and counsel he may use in enacting laws.

XIV. Laws must be equitable and beneficial to the Republic; they should be concise and strong. For it is not easy to add a reason to a law.

XV. The execution of the law occurs when the prince either grants rewards to the observers or inflicts punishment on the transgressors. Hence, all the force and authority of the law depend on this.

XVI. When the meaning of the law is doubtful, it is the prince's duty to interpret it based on diverse reasons, times, persons, and other circumstances, and to adapt it to public use.

XVII. And if a prince has the power to abrogate laws, he should not, however, arbitrarily change those which have been established by law or by custom, which have the force of law; but only if the law contains manifest injustice or is harmful to the Republic.

7:

On Advisors
and Other Ministers of the Kingdom

I. Since a prince cannot alone establish everything, nor can he be present in all parts of his principate, it is necessary for him to employ ministers whose services he may use either in seeking counsel or in managing affairs.

II. The prince should choose ministers who are good, loyal, and experienced. For the governance of the prince is generally as the ministers are. However, it is not easy to assign many offices to one person.

III. Ministers can either be for counsel (these are called Councilors) or for managing affairs.

IV. Even if the prince is most knowledgeable about his own matters, he should not easily undertake anything of great importance without first consulting his councilors, and doing so with care, lest necessity drive him to hastily seek counsel.

V. Two things must be considered in councilors: First, what qualities they should possess; and second, how they should be utilized.

VI. Much depends on the selection of councilors. So much so that it is debatable whether it is more tolerable for a kingdom to be under a good prince with bad councilors, than the opposite. Certainly, if the prince is not an absolute monarch and is not considered malicious, cunning, or obstinate, but simple and rather unfit to govern, it is more tolerable to have a prince who is effeminate than councilors. But if the prince is an absolute monarch, it would be said that he is a bad prince who is malicious and cunning, and matters would be viewed in the opposite way.

VII. Councilors should be natives rather than foreigners, unless their services are needed from outside. They should be older rather than younger: however, it is useful for young people to participate in councils, provided that it is not confidential, not to cast votes, but to listen.

VIII. Councilors should be wise; that is, they should be knowledgeable about political matters, not only in general but also in specifics. They should understand the character and morals of their prince, and be conversant with foreign nations.

IX. Furthermore, they should be pious, honest, and supportive of the Republic; they should be strong, temperate, and serious; not contentious or arrogant. They should calmly bear the opinions of those with whom they disagree, and should not dismiss counsel indiscriminately, especially if it does not come from their own authority. They should be frank, and express their opinion freely, whether it is agreeable to the prince or not. Above all, they should not be flatterers; they should finally be taciturn and faithful.

X. Since good councilors are rare, the prince should not appoint anyone to this role lightly unless he has diligently inquired into their nature, character, intelligence, and morals.

XI. The councilors may be chosen from various groups of people, but especially from the nobility and the learned. The prince should establish distinct ranks of councilors among them, and have some closer, others less intimate; but all should be bound to him by oath.

XII. Regarding the election: concerning the use of councilors, the following must be noted. First, the prince himself must be present in consultations: both to prevent disputes and to encourage the good to remain loyal, and to diminish the bad by his presence.

XIII. Councilors are permitted to express their opinions freely; thereafter, the prince should weigh them. He should not reveal his own opinion, nor show in which direction he leans. If some counsel leads to bad results, the councilors should not be blamed; for sound counsel is more praiseworthy when combined with reason than reckless counsel that happens to have a favorable outcome.

XIV. The prince must take care not to have any of his councilors so obnoxious that he manages everything by their nod.

XV. It is beneficial for the prince to have councilors in neighboring regions, from whom he can be informed about all matters occurring there.

XVI. There is a difference between perpetual council and occasional council. I call perpetual council that which the prince always has in his court. I call occasional council that which is summoned at specified times, convening the principal nobles and orders of the kingdom. Such council is often called an assembly.

XVII. To convene assemblies pertains to the prince, or to him who has authority. However, in the state of a monarchy, it should be frequent, lest anything be lost from the majesty of the state.

XVIII. The prince should designate the time and place of the assembly, and take care that the matters of deliberation are communicated to all orders and members of the assembly. He should attend the assembly, propose the topics, and speak about them if necessary.

XIX. This covers councilors: next, we follow ministers for conducting affairs, and these are of various kinds. Some are public, others are court officials. The chief public ministers include the Chancellor, governors of provinces, presiding officers of public courts, commanders, tribunes of cavalry, and infantry; lesser ones include secretaries, scribes, centurions, and court officials, such as the palatine prince, that is, the chief steward of the court, marshals of the court, chamberlains, etc.

XX. These offices can vary in such a way that a certain order cannot be established. For each Republic has certain offices that are proper to it.

XXI. Of all these, one thing can be noted: that primary offices should be assigned to the nobles and the great; not to the common people, unless individual virtue distinguishes them.

XXII. It is also useful for the prince to have emissaries so that he may learn the minds and morals of his subjects; but so that they may not reveal themselves to the subjects, and that the prince should not readily trust informers, nor condemn anyone solely for the reports of informers.

8:

On the Birth, Education, and Burial of Subjects

I. There is hardly anything for which a prince should care more than for his subjects. For if the subjects are well, the entire Republic will easily be prosperous. Among subjects, many things must be considered; we will give first place to birth, education, and burial.

II. To ensure nothing is amiss in birth, certain laws must be established regarding the entering into marriage. For it is not permitted for anyone to marry or for anyone to wed just anyone. Consideration must be given not only to status or fortune but also to virtue and age.

III. No one is permitted to procure an abortion, much less to expose or kill newborn infants; such acts should be punished as atrocious crimes. Care must be taken to attend diligently to the legitimate births of children, and all means should be employed to prevent the Republic from being filled with illegitimate and spurious children. To prevent this, spurious children should not easily be elevated to dignities.

IV. Public authority should also establish expert and trustworthy midwives, and they should be instructed to record the names of the fathers of the children born, if they have no husbands.

V. Thus, we have addressed birth; we now turn to education, which is so necessary in the Republic that without it all magistrates are carelessly incompetent.

VI. Boys should be educated at home until the age of seven; after that, the care of parents should be combined with the public care of the prince, and public institutions. Nor should it be free for parents to either entrust their children to public discipline or not.

VII. For this purpose, colleges, gymnasiums, and schools must be established for all liberal arts; and the revenues pertaining to them should be arranged. Moreover, wise men should be selected who may undertake this duty under public authority, so that the youth are well-instructed.

VIII. Boys and girls must be educated. The education of boys pertains either to the body or to the mind. The education of the body should be such that boys learn to endure labor, and that their bodies are exercised for agility and strength; so that they can provide for themselves if necessary; or for military purposes.

IX. The prince should establish gymnasiums where all honorable exercises are prescribed, which prepare youths for war.

X. The education of the mind concerns either the intellect or morals. The mind should be imbued with knowledge of languages, arts, and liberal sciences. However, care should be taken in this matter. For it should not be directed towards the study of letters unless those suitable for this are found; the others should learn practical trades, commerce, or military discipline. No one should be in the Republic for nothing, nor should they be allowed to beg for alms.

XI. The arts for girls are reading, writing, arithmetic, sewing, and so forth, which they should learn in separate gymnasiums, from respectable and dignified matrons appointed by the prince. The morals or virtues common to both should be established.

XII. So that citizens are well-mannered, all virtues should be publicly commanded, and contrary vices should be prohibited and restrained, with established penalties.

XIII. Nor should it be sufficient for the prince to ensure that the subjects live according to ethical precepts; he must also ensure that they observe economic and political precepts. Especially those that pertain to the Republic, so that subjects are strong, temperate, generous, modest, just, and that they diligently avoid contrary vices; but this also pertains to the happiness of the Republic, so that subjects prudently manage their households, live in harmony, avoid quarrels, and as many other similar things as possible.

9:

On the Maintenance of Sustenance and Health, Burial, and Other Matters Pertaining to the Happiness of Citizens

I. Having addressed the birth and education of subjects, we now proceed to discuss sustenance and the care of provisions.

II. In order to avoid difficulties with provisions in the Republic, provisions for the supply of food should be established, and ministers should be appointed to oversee all matters that could either harm or benefit the provisions.

III. The duties of these overseers are as follows: First, to ensure the proper measure and weight are observed, and to investigate; thus, punishing those who use unfair measures. Then, to ensure that fields are diligently cultivated, proposing rewards or exemptions from taxes for a few years, either to drain swamps or to till barren fields, and to remove the impediments that hinder the laborers from working the fields. Thirdly, to establish the price of provisions, and to ensure no one may raise it at their own discretion.

IV. The prince should ensure that goods brought in from elsewhere are transported easily and safely, and also that they can be easily exported if there are any surpluses in the Republic.

V. To prevent public scarcity or famine, granaries should be established, in which only as much grain is collected as is judged sufficient for the annual necessities of the populace.

VI. When necessity presses, no grain should be exported. No one should have more grain than necessary; the surplus should be sold at a fair price, or reluctantly. Those who falsely deal with grain should be severely punished.

VII. If necessity presses strongly, public grain should be distributed among families, given for free to the poor, or at a low price to the wealthy, in moderation.

VIII. Thus, concerning sustenance; but also regarding health, there should be care taken: for which purpose both Aediles and Physicians should be appointed.

IX. The duty of the Aediles is to ensure that nothing putrid or foul exists in the city, nor should corrupt meats or fish be sold, from which either the air might be contaminated or disease might arise.

X. Physicians should be appointed who are skilled and faithful, and those who deceive and cheat should be punished.

XI. The duty of physicians is not only to cure the sick but also to oversee the pharmacies with public authority to ensure that no corrupt medicines are used.

XII. During a plague, efforts must be made to prevent contagion as much as possible.

XIII. Those who wish to escape contagion should be free to do so, except for those who must remain for the sake of public duty.

XIV. Furthermore, these matters pertain to the lives of subjects; we now follow what must be preserved regarding burial.

XV. First, the prince should properly establish those matters pertaining to burial; and should take care that the goods of the deceased are preserved intact for lawful heirs, even if they are far away; which should not only pertain to citizens but also to foreigners, even if in France and elsewhere it is the custom for the property of foreigners to be seized if they die without a testament, even for their own children.

XVI. The bodies of the dead should often be removed from the crowd of the living so that they may not harm others; and preferably in the morning rather than at another time.

XVII. Corpses should not be buried too quickly nor too slowly. Funeral processions should be conducted moderately; nor should anyone be allowed to be buried with their treasures.

XVIII. All these things are indeed necessary so that subjects may live comfortably and honorably; it remains for us to add certain things that pertain to splendor and delight.

XIX. For this purpose, it is required that the honor and splendor of illustrious families be maintained in posterity; and that distinguished individuals from abroad also sustain their dignity through their appearance, sustenance, and attire.

XX. If noble foreigners visit, they should be well-mannered, and equipped with suitable expenses, so that their house may reflect their splendor. Otherwise, it will happen that they will disgrace their own lineage.

XXI. Additionally, for the delight of the subjects, it seems appropriate that the prince provide or at least indulge in certain types of public games and feasts; but he should set a limit to these.

10:

On the Ranks and Community of Citizens

I. What we have discussed in the previous chapter pertains to individual citizens; now it follows that we examine the ranks of citizens and their community.

II. We will consider ranks with regard to dignity, offices, and benefits.

III. The highest rank is that of Duke; following this are: 2. Marquess, 3. Landgrave, 4. Count, 5. Baron, 6. Noble, and finally the common people, each according to their rank, which varies greatly, such as merchants, soldiers, farmers, craftsmen, and so on.

IV. Just as subjects are distinguished by ranks, it is expedient for the Republic that distinct methods of economic management be established. Nor should it be allowed for a noble to imitate a baron in matters of his finances; nor for a baron to imitate a count, except in the opposite way if poverty demands it.

V. Regarding offices, they should be granted by the prince not for price, but for merit. For it is both disgraceful and dangerous to sell offices of the Republic.

VI. The prince should diligently protect the dignity, authority, and privileges of his ministers, and he should investigate their administration and offenses.

VII. Moreover, there are various offices in each Republic, and their names and laws should be derived from the description of each public matter.

VIII. There are also beneficiaries, who are called vassals; their benefits are referred to by the term "feud" in Longobardic, not in Latin.

IX. A fief is land or another immovable possession free from taxes, which someone holds by the prince's grant, whereby they are obliged to loyalty and to provide military service to the prince in times of war.

X. If a beneficiary breaks the pledged loyalty to the lord and fails to assist him in peril, or if his dignity has not been maintained according to his abilities, he loses his benefits by that very right.

XI. Nor are subjects only bound to pledge loyalty in the name of the fief, which they call homage; but the prince himself, not inasmuch as he is a prince, but inasmuch as he possesses lands situated under another prince's authority.

XII. Thus, we have discussed ranks; next follows the community of subjects, whether in neighborhoods or villages, or in cities, or in guilds.

XIII. The term "families" is mentioned in economic discussions. This should be held particularly in mind; it pertains to the prince to preserve the ancient dignity of illustrious families and to transmit all rights and privileges which are due to virtue to their descendants.

XIV. In this community, however, women should not be counted, since they transition from their native family to that of their husbands.

XV. Villages and neighborhoods throughout the Republic should be numerous, not only for the convenience of those who live there, but especially for the cultivation of fields.

XVI. As a community, certain rights should be granted to villages, and officers or praetors should know about minor cases; more serious cases, especially capital ones, should be reserved for cities.

XVII. Therefore, urban community is more necessary for the happiness of the Republic because it is also larger. The place, persons, and rights must be inspected.

XVIII. A city should be established in a healthy and safe location; additionally, it should be fertile, especially if it is in a low-lying area. For fertility can easily compensate for business activities if they are maritime.

XIX. Whether it is advisable to fortify cities cannot be affirmed without distinction. For a fortress is necessary if there is a distrust of the subjects, or if cities cannot be adequately fortified without one. If the cities are strong and the subjects loyal, a fortress does not seem necessary.

XX. The persons considered in this society are citizens, that is, those who enjoy the same rights of liberty and the same privileges and benefits. In this commonality of civil rights, some are born, others are adopted. And although both are citizens, there should still be some distinction between native citizens and those adopted.

XXI. The rights of cities are very varied, and are almost specific to each. In general, it can be observed that it is very necessary for the prince to protect urban communities and their rights and privileges. For cities are the cultivators of conveniences, arts, and virtues; they are the workshops of wealth, and sanctuaries for activities during war, and fortifications for the Republic.

XXII. Finally, associations in the Republic should either be established or permitted, whether they are political, ecclesiastical, or even for merchants or craftsmen. Gatherings and clandestine assemblies should be strictly prohibited.

XXIII. In all associations, except for the entertainment of games (which I will omit), the prince should preside, either personally or through a legate; or at least should oversee what takes place there.

11:

On Judicial Processes and Censorship

I. In order that all these matters which we have hitherto prescribed may be more easily obtained in the Republic, a judicial system is required to promote the inclination towards virtue and to curb the malice of the wicked.

II. Judicial processes can be either forensic or censorial. Forensic matters pertain either to rewards and punishments or to disputes.

III. Forensic trials should be conducted publicly, to restrain the wickedness of judges and the audacity of subjects, and to secure authority for matters adjudicated.

IV. In awarding rewards and punishments, the prince, or those who act in the prince's place, should be prudent and just. If punishment is to be administered, it is preferable to lack in rewards than to lack in punishments.

V. In place of rewards, either wealth is granted or honor. And wealth should indeed be granted sparingly, so that the public treasury is not exhausted; however, there should also be moderation in honors, lest honors, easily obtained, become trivial or the subjects become insolent by receiving excessive honors.

VI. These rewards can vary in rank, through which distinction is made. For either a commoner is adorned with nobility, or a noble is created a Baron, and so forth. The same applies to offices and military honors, and elsewhere.

VII. These rewards are ordinary. An extraordinary reward is called a privilege. This can be either personal or real.

VIII. A personal privilege is one that is granted to only one person, so that it does not extend to the whole of their family or heirs. A real privilege pertains to the whole family and extends to the heirs.

IX. Privileges consist either in immunity from the burdens of the Republic or in the enjoyment of something that has been granted as a benefit. However, privileges can be granted to individuals or entire communities.

X. In administering punishments, care must be taken that they correspond to the crimes and persons, and that there is no exception made for individuals: and if an entire community is to be punished, it should be done so that the example of the punishment pertains to all; severity should apply to a few.

XI. Such punishment is often called decimation.

XII. Disputes can arise either between a magistrate and subjects or between subjects.

XIII. Even if the monarch does not easily allow himself to be moved by disputes from subjects, if a dispute cannot be avoided, he should convene the principal nobles of the kingdom, who should determine the arising dispute without prejudice to the majesty of the state.

XIV. It should not be permitted for subjects to litigate frivolously; if there is a just or at least a probable cause for litigation, it is best that the entire matter be settled by arbitrators to avoid the burdens of litigation. If this is not possible, it must be settled in a public trial.

XV. In judicial matters, the judge, the prosecutor, the defendant, and the administrators of justice are to be considered.

XVI. Judges should vary in their ranks; but within each rank, there should be few, who are knowledgeable, honest, and wise, free from bias, and endowed with authority, so that if anyone disregards their opinion, they may manage the case.

XVII. A judge should decide according to the facts and evidence; if he wishes to follow conscience against what appears in court, he should resign from the judge's role and become a witness.

XVIII. The actor is he who accuses or petitions; the defendant is he who defends. The cause of this actor is always favored more than that of the defendant.

XIX. The forensic administrators are the summoned, the notaries, and the scribes. Their duties and salaries should be duly established, and serious attention must be given to them, in whatever manner they exceed their prescribed limits.

XX. The course of a judicial process should not extend over a long period. For this matter is very burdensome and harmful to subjects.

XXI. The parts of a trial are citation, preparation, litigation contest, dispute over the cause, in which are contained exceptions, replies, and counter-replies, the production of witnesses or documents, conclusion or verdict, and execution.

XXII. Trials can either be civil or criminal. In criminal trials, the actor is the representative of the Republic; in civil matters, it is a private individual who has been offended.

XXIII. The more serious the crime, the more the criminal trials consist of arrest, custody, inquiry, and punishment.

XXIV. In order for criminals to be captured, it is not enough to merely establish asylums; unless they can be proven innocent, those who have committed offenses should not be overlooked, especially not against a magistrate, but rather against those who may wish to seek retribution for an injury received.

XXV. Custody serves more to detain than to punish, unless someone has been sentenced to prison by the judgment of the judges. Therefore, detainees should be cared for in custody, so they do not suffer punishment before sentencing. However, prisons must be well-maintained, so that those detained do not escape.

XXVI. Inquiry can be verbal or by torture. Inquiry through torture should not easily be applied, but only when those manifestly stubborn refuse to confess their crimes.

XXVII. The punishment varies: fines, confiscation of all property, perpetual imprisonment, exile, condemnation to public works, whipping, death; and these, too, are varied. However, of all, the most approved should be those that are both shameful and less harsh.

XXVIII. However, because many are by nature external, and cannot be prescribed by political laws, they therefore do not fall under judicial forensics; thus, a censorial judgment seems appropriate. For censorship is the most useful safeguard against many vices, which cannot otherwise be restrained.

XXIX. Censorship should be enforced for heinous private crimes; such as excess in food and clothing, in feasts, and in entertainments; as well as the disputes of spouses, and in the obedience of children to parents and masters towards servants; as well as discord among citizens.

XXX. No one is exempt from censure, except for the prince. For the prince must be admonished if he is to be held accountable for his duties, if he commits an offense; he should also be subject to censure.

XXXI. The duty of the censor should be exercised by the prince himself; for this purpose, grave and honest men should be appointed, endowed with the highest authority; among whom the citizenry should be distributed (if it is larger) according to a certain number of families that should be observed.

12:

On Public Revenues

I. Money is not only the nerve of war but of the entire Republic. Therefore, the prince must diligently work to be equipped with ample resources to cover the expenses necessary for governance and judgment, as well as for waging war if needed; and from God, that nothing be lacking for public or private uses.

II. At this point, two things must be observed: the method of acquiring money and the method of spending it for suitable uses.

III. Money is collected in three primary ways: from coinage, from taxes, and from levies or tributes.

IV. The right to mint money is considered among the rights of majesty. Therefore, it should be permitted to no one except the prince. If anyone usurps this right, he should be judged guilty of high treason.

V. The material for the coin should have a specific weight; it should be minted, stamped, and should conform to what is established by the public authority of the prince.

VI. The price of the currency, once established, should not be increased or decreased at the discretion of the subjects; it should be stable and permanent.

VII. Any profit the prince may derive from monetary matters should be small. For if the price of the currency is set much higher than the value of the raw material, it poses a danger that subjects or foreigners may counterfeit the currency.

VIII. Counterfeiters of currency should be punished severely. Moreover, foreign coins should not be admitted unless necessity demands it.

IX. A tax is that which the magistrate collects from commerce, that is, from the sale of goods that are sold, imported, or exported.

X. When imposing taxes, the magistrate should be fair, so that commerce is neither impeded nor transferred elsewhere.

XI. Custom officers or publicans should be established, who, at their own risk, should collect certain taxes each year; and this should be done according to a fixed law that determines what is to be charged for various goods, with penalties added for those who defraud the publicans.

XII. A tribute is what subjects owe from their possessions; in Latin, it is called "collatio."

XIII. It is necessary to maintain a proper balance, so that either subjects are not drained, or the prince is not rendered odious. The balance should be either greater or lesser, as necessity demands.

XIV. It is beneficial that the tribute be derived from those goods that affect the poor the least, namely, not from necessities of life, but from those pertaining to pleasure, luxury, splendor, etc.

XV. Furthermore, the tribute can be derived from immovable property, such as estates, fields, etc., or from movable property.

XVI. In order for the tribute on immovable property to be fair, the prince should ensure that the immovable assets of all subjects are listed in catalogs, so that a census can be established that responds to both quantity and quality, imposing it on each.

XVII. This also pertains to tithes, which are taken from grain: likewise, from the sale of immovable property, and from those who build within the Republic, etc.

XVIII. Three main types of taxation are established: Juggling (Jugatio), Capitation (Capitatio), and Hospitality (Hóspitatio).

XIX. Juggling is imposed based on the magnitude, number, and quality of the lands. It is called "per jugerum" (per acre).

XX. Capitation is that which is established on individual persons' heads, regardless of their wealth.

XXI. Hospitality is when subjects are compelled to provide hospitality to soldiers or courtiers.

XXII. These are indeed the primary methods of acquiring revenues; there may also be other subsidiary methods, such as through the prince's increase of wealth from dowries, inheritance, gifts, alluvion, etc.

XXIII. The prince should diligently ensure that collected revenues are gathered, preserved, and prudently dispensed, and this should be done through trustworthy individuals who should report annually on all accounts. For nothing is more harmful than to trust revenue management too securely to administrators.

XXIV. All revenues should serve the prince, both for paying the stipends of soldiers and officials, as well as for private uses. Although it seems less envy-inducing, if revenues are distinctly used for private purposes, they should be distinguished from those that are spent for the Republic.

13:

On Defending, Augmenting,
and Beautifying the Republic

I. The prince should strive to assist in these revenues, first to defend and protect the Republic, and then also to augment and adorn it.

II. However, the prince should defend the Republic against all evils that can be avoided by human industry. For those evils which are beyond human foresight are left to God and nature; such as excessive rains, lightning, violent winds, hail, droughts, earthquakes, and similar matters.

III. Matters that can at least partially be avoided through human foresight are quite varied. The first that comes to mind is the inundation of the sea or rivers and fires.

IV. Flooding should be contained by dikes and other fortifications. Fires should be either prevented or extinguished.

V. To facilitate fire prevention, buildings in cities should not be made of straw, but of tiles; there should also be night watchmen who call out in case of a fire, should any be spotted.

VI. A certain arrangement of ladders and buckets should be established to extinguish fires. Then, porters, sailors, and others appointed by public authority should be required to act promptly in extinguishing fires.

VII. Arsonists should also be punished severely.

VIII. The second defense is against famine, which we have previously discussed. The third is against harmful wild animals, bears, wolves, boars, and similar creatures. This is addressed by hunting, which the prince should oversee from time to time.

IX. The primary defense should be taken against men, such as against seditious men, robbers, pirates, bandits, and similar others, all of whom should be kept as far from their borders as possible: armed men should be chosen to investigate them. Most importantly, defenses must be prepared against enemies.

X. For this reason, it is necessary that fortified cities and castles exist within the Republic's borders; and especially that the gates be fortified. This is not only necessary to fend off enemies, but also to prevent anyone from fleeing the Republic or exporting things that should not be exported. It also seems useful for the prince to maintain soldiers in border cities or ports.

XI. Furthermore, the prince should strive to maintain the reputation and resources of his subjects. Therefore, he should prohibit libelous pamphlets and satires against individuals; also usurers, dishonest moneylenders, extortionists, etc., who drain the populace of their wealth.

XII. No one should be allowed to practice alchemical arts; those who act against the law should be prosecuted, especially if they have suffered from misfortune.

XIII. The prince should not permit beggars, whom the Lombards call "dani," but the magistrates should grant aid to the needy with moderate sums.

XIV. Regarding the amplification of the Republic, the prince should not be overly solicitous; for it is unjust and dangerous to invade the lands of others. However, if someone has been repelled in a just war, he is permitted not only to defend his own borders but also to invade others.

XV. The beautification of the Republic, as it is neither unjust nor dangerous, should be attended to with diligence. Beautification consists of the splendor and utility of public works, from which some benefit returns to private citizens.

14:

On the Prince's Court

I. The prince should primarily take care of the Republic, but he should not entirely neglect his private affairs, nor those of his court.

II. The private care or court of the prince involves either persons or things. Among persons, just as the head of the household is the first and principal caretaker, so should he be.

III. For the security of the body, he should have bodyguards, and indeed from the people whom he governs, so that he does not appear to distrust his own subjects.

IV. He should also have faithful cooks, tasters, and purveyors.

V. The second care is of the spouse; he should manage her so that she is not excessively extravagant: he should remove examples and temptations of immorality from the women's quarters, and not easily trust her in confidential matters, nor permit her any part of the governance.

VI. The third care is for offspring, whom he should have suckled either by their mother or by some illustrious nurse, who possesses virtuous qualities.

VII. He should ensure that male offspring are educated by masters and tutors of such morals that they fill their minds with virtue.

VIII. In forming alliances, the prince should choose such noblemen who will be beneficial to the Republic.

IX. He should not only provide sustenance for his brothers, ensuring an honorable and dignified support for his family, but he should also entrust them with positions or dignities if he has tested their loyalty.

X. He should honorably arrange marriages for his sisters, adding a dowry, but one that does not detract from the Republic.

XI. After blood relatives, officials follow: the prince should not increase their number excessively, but should maintain his court as much as possible by dignity and merit.

XII. The primary duties of his court should be assigned to the needy rather than to outsiders. The principal officials are the Prefect of the Court, or Palatine, the Marshal, the Master of the Household, the Chamberlains, the Burggrave, or those who govern the lesser officials of the court, the Master of Supplies, and so forth.

XIII. The less important officials include the chamberlains, cooks, stewards, etc.

XIV. All of these should be appointed by the prince either through selection or prudent governance, ensuring they are reputable and honest; for the behavior of courtiers often reflects on the prince, and the morals of courtiers can easily become public knowledge.

XV. In diet, clothing, and salaries or allowances, the prince should not be too frugal, nor too extravagant.

XVI. The things the prince should take care of are either the palace or the furnishings. And all these should be splendid and neat.

15:

On Foreigners, and on Legates and Envoys

I. Foreigners should be considered in two ways, namely, whether they are in the kingdom, where they either wander or reside, or whether they are outside the kingdom.

II. Regarding foreigners, officials should be appointed in the borders, particularly in the royal regions or other fortified places, to observe incoming foreigners.

III. It should also be ensured that the routes for travelers are safe and that hospices are convenient, nor should it be permitted for locals to drain foreigners.

IV. They should ward off those little wanderers, whom they call Nubians and Cygars, either as scouts or as wandering bandits.

V. If princes themselves enter the kingdom, they should be received by the prince and honored as they depart. Others, who are of lower rank, should be attended to by court officials as they arrive or leave.

VI. If any foreigners wish to settle in the Republic, the prince should not hinder them if they are virtuous men, or if they were banished from their homeland through no fault of their own. However, those justly exiled for significant reasons should not be admitted.

VII. However, citizenship should not easily be granted to foreigners, but only when manifestly required by the utility of the Republic. Otherwise, the matter would not be without risk.

VIII. Furthermore, foreigners should be restrained by certain laws from doing anything against the Republic.

IX. Honors, magistracies, and noble insignia should not easily be bestowed upon foreigners, even if they are noble in their own country. Even less should they be allowed to exercise private jurisdiction.

X. The Jews should not be received into the Republic unless under certain conditions. First, they must adhere to the laws of the state, like other citizens, and live quietly and without scandal. Second, they should not contract marriages with Christians. Third, they must not entice Christians to their religion. Fourth, they should not practice usury excessively. Fifth, they must not speak ill of Christ or Christians. Sixth, they must not impede any Jew wishing to convert to Christianity.

XI. Foreigners outside the kingdom follow, with whom the prince usually establishes treaties and alliances.

XII. In all these matters, the prince should aim to maintain peace and establish good relations with neighboring princes; and he should carefully uphold the honor of his nation with outsiders.

XIII. This can indeed be done either through letters or through appointed ministers. What can be conveyed conveniently, safely, and honorably through letters should not be achieved without the presence of envoys.

XIV. In these matters, the prince should have certain letter formulas and the appropriate titles for each prince; he should use reliable secretaries and couriers, and also utilize confidential notes in his letters.

XV. Appointed ministers may be either acting envoys or legates; and the only difference between them is that envoys are usually more solemn.

XVI. The acting ministers may be either public or secret. They utilize this to be aware of what is being conducted in other kingdoms.

XVII. In sending legates, the most careful selection must be made: they should be chosen who can benefit the Republic and its honor. For this purpose, wisdom, eloquence, grace, language proficiency, etc., are required.

XVIII. The legate should be equipped with letters of credence. He should also have a prescribed method of action. Nor should he exceed the limits of his mandate, unless in the utmost and swiftest necessity.

XIX. Among other things, he should have in his mandate that he does not accept gifts from the prince to whom he is sent, except those which are manifestly public honors.

XX. It is not only necessary to send legates, but also to admit those who are sent by other princes.

XXI. The prince should promptly demand letters of credence from the legates after receiving them. Once read, he should grant them appropriate honor and ensure their person is sacred and inviolable. If, however, they have conspired against the Republic, they should be restrained.

XXII. The prince should himself hear the legates, either in person or through trustworthy interpreters.

XXIII. Treaties or alliances with neighbors may be of various types: some involve mere proximity and some involve friendship, loyalty, and mutual aid.

XXIV. The closer a neighboring nation is, the more cautious the prince should be. And if peace can be achieved on equitable terms, it is safest; if it cannot, he should fortify the borders well.

XXV. The boundaries of jurisdiction should be fixed and certain; if any dispute arises about them, it should be resolved swiftly.

XXVI. In tighter alliances, the prince should be most cautious, for such matters are extremely risky on both sides, whether alliances are formed or not.

XXVII. Most perilous are those alliances made by weaker states with stronger ones.

XXVIII. Less perilous are alliances made solely for the sake of trade; more dangerous are those formed for the sake of defense; and most dangerous are those formed for the sake of offense.

16:

On War

I. However, peace is far more to be desired than war; nevertheless, times and causes arise which make war necessary and just. Therefore, discussions about war are also crucial for politics.

II. Although wars can be justly waged for either offensive or defensive causes, yet, according to natural law, offense aligns more closely with justice than defense. An offense can never be just unless it is to repel a harm or injury inflicted upon the Republic.

III. Therefore, these two provide a just cause for undertaking war: to defend the Republic and to repel harm or injury; or to retain one's own and to recover what has been lost. If the prince cannot achieve his goals through other means, he must resort to war and take up arms for the defense of the Republic; indeed, even for offense, if his strength supports it. If it does not support it, it is better to conceal the injury than to create the risk of greater harm by seeking revenge.

IV. In order to proceed in this matter, six main points should be discussed: 1. The gods, who precede the war. 2. The resources through which war is waged. 3. The actual waging of war. 4. The adjuncts of war. 5. The effects and consequences. 6. Lastly, the types of war.

V. Regarding the first point, the prince should ensure that his subjects are exercised in arms during peacetime and prepared for war. For it is much safer for subjects to be trained than to rely on foreign soldiers.

VI. However, if the subjects are seditious, the prince should not permit them the use of arms; much less should he allow them to be trained in arms.

VII. Not only should the subjects be trained in the handling of arms, but they should also be accustomed to labor, hardships, and military duties, as necessary, when other matters require it; in brief, they should be prepared for all military responsibilities.

VIII. Before the prince decides to go to war, he should invoke the divine name and deliberate correctly about all matters, assessing his own strength and that of the enemy, and directing his council to ensure nothing unexpected occurs.

IX. If after all these assessments the prince decides that war must be waged, he should announce it either personally (which is commonly known as a declaration of war) or by letters. For it is not honorable for a prince to launch a war without any such thought. In defensive wars, a declaration is not required.

X. Next, we consider the resources through which war is conducted. These are fourfold: Persons, Resources, Counsel, and Military Discipline.

XI. The principal person is the prince himself. For since he necessarily must be the head in war, who has absolute power, it is not safe to grant this power to anyone else.

XII. If, however, the prince cannot participate in the war, he should appoint a legate for himself, a native, loyal, strong, cautious person, endowed with authority and grace.

XIII. Other military personnel serving the prince are called soldiers. Soldiers are usually recruited in two ways: The first way is when a trumpet or drum calls the people together so that those who wish to be soldiers can have their names recorded; the second way is when the enemy suddenly attacks, and the populace is summoned by the sound of bells or some other signal to defend themselves.

XIV. Soldiers, if possible, should be gathered from rugged places, who are strong in body and spirit, and of proven morals; and this should be done in a certain number, to avoid either too great a multitude or too few, which could be detrimental.

XV. The recruited soldiers should be carefully examined, and the unfit dismissed, while the others are entered into a roster, distributed into classes, and sworn in.

XVI. A certain form of the oath should be established and expressed, so that the soldiers promise that they will obey the commander and maintain military discipline.

XVII. A soldier may be either cavalry or infantry. Each is necessary for conducting war. Although in battles fought in open places cavalry may seem to be preferred, in mountainous locations and from the perspective of the overall conduct of war, infantry is considered more advantageous.

XVIII. Not only should regular soldiers be used, but also auxiliaries, when necessity demands; these may be either native or foreign. However, there is some risk associated with a large number of foreign soldiers, especially if they belong to the same nation and have a leader who is bound by oath to a foreign prince.

XIX. Soldiers may be either common troops or officers, and the multitude and diversity of the officers should be determined more by experience than by precepts.

XX. In addition to soldiers, many other persons are necessary in war, namely advisors, treasury officials, the supreme judge of capital matters, as well as the commander of supplies, the commander of armaments, chariots, ships, bridges, and so forth. This should include a certain number of persons sufficient to provide for supplies, transport, etc.

XXI. Thus regarding persons: next come the resources, primarily animals, horses, and where necessary, camels and elephants.

XXII. After animals, livestock follows, which is truly the lifeblood of war.

XXIII. Third in importance is logistics, for which the commander must take great care.

XXIV. Logistics pertains either to supplies for people or for horses and other draft animals.

XXV. Fourthly, weapons are required, with which the soldiers should be equipped. To ensure this, the soldiers' arms should often be inspected.

XXVI. In addition to arms, other instruments, tents, chariots, ships, bridges, axes, spades, etc., are also required.

XXVII. The arms and attire of soldiers should not be too expensive, so that they do not attract the enemy's attention during the battle.

XXVIII. Next come the counsels, which were required in the resources of waging war. Military counsel may be straightforward and without deceit; or indirect, and associated with deceit. This involves stratagems, reconnaissance, securing betrayal, managing relationships with enemies, interception, deceit, and delay. All these are permitted and commendable, provided they are conducted safely.

XXIX. Finally, military discipline is required, which is contained in laws and their execution. First, effort should be made so that soldiers, as much as possible, conduct themselves according to ethical, economic, and political laws, which pertain to nature and nations.

XXX. Then they should be bound by specific laws that pertain solely to military service, which command them to live quietly and peacefully, to abstain from riots and seditions; to guard their arms diligently; to act bravely in battle; to keep their oaths: with capital punishment established for those who flee to the enemy, who avoid fighting, or who desert.

XXXI. The judgment regarding soldiers' offenses should be brief; the punishment should be strict and respond to the laws. Yet it should vary according to the severity of the offenses.

17:

On Belligerance,
and on the Adjuncts and Effects of War

I. In the third section, we propose to discuss the belligerence itself. Here, it should first be observed that all opportunities to harm the enemy should be seized and anticipated.

II. In war, we will first consider the mobilization of the army, second the positioning, third the assault, fourth the engagement, and fifth the siege.

III. When mobilizing the army, it must be deliberated whether it is more expedient for the enemy to await the limits of your domain or to invade another territory.

IV. Moreover, whoever leads the army must consider whether it is his own territory or that of an ally, but he should be careful not to harm the locals or to trouble them. In enemy territory, soldiers may plunder, but not recklessly, lest they be surrounded by treachery.

V. If you allow any army to cross through your territory (which must sometimes be done), all must be diligently fortified.

VI. The location through which the army is to march should be explored, to determine whether it is forested, mountainous, flat, narrow, broad, passable, or obstructed by rivers and other impediments.

VII. For the positioning, a suitable location must be chosen, one that is convenient for supplies, difficult for the enemy to assault, and not harmful to those already present. The form should be suited to the natural location and adjusted to the number of soldiers. Areas should be specifically assigned for cavalry and infantry, all arranged in the appropriate proportion.

VIII. If the siege is likely to be prolonged, the army must be moved into winter quarters, so that the comforts of the camps do not too heavily burden the soldiers. However, these discomforts must be endured if there is a risk of invasion by an enemy prepared to attack.

IX. The assault against the enemy should not easily be made unless the enemy is terrified, or is secure and unprepared. For if the enemy is prepared and defends strongly, the defending parts are more advantageous than those attacking.

X. A minor engagement is called skirmishing. If a proper army is assembled, it is called a battle. Before reaching a proper battle, it is useful to send out a few soldiers for skirmishing purposes; this serves to explore the enemy's strength, or to discover or boost the morale of the soldiers.

XI. A battle should not be incited arbitrarily by an enemy provocatively challenging; rather, it should be undertaken with regard to location, timing, and other conditions of opportunity. The commander should encourage the soldiers with a determined countenance and appropriate speech: he should cut off hope for retreat. He himself should be present in battle; nothing ignites soldiers' virtue more than the presence of their leader. A legate should be assigned to the leader, who, should the leader fall, continues the battle.

XII. During battle, nothing adverse should be signaled to the soldiers but should be cautiously concealed. If anything advantageous occurs, it should be further encouraged and made known to the soldiers to bolster their courage.

XIII. The commander should place a select few soldiers in ambush, to launch a surprise attack on the enemy with all their might. This is of utmost importance for victory. Meanwhile, the commander should be wary of the enemy's ambushes.

XIV. If victory is obtained, the soldiers should not scatter too quickly after the engagement to seize spoils; nor should they rashly pursue the fleeing enemy; for a single fall can always deprive the defeated of hope for salvation.

XV. If the enemy should escape victorious, the army should regroup in a safe location with their formations intact. For it is no lesser art to withdraw a defeated army than to conquer.

XVI. A siege should either be initiated or maintained. For when a city or fortress is besieged, it must be known precisely how much the enemy has in supplies and how long they can hold out if fortified so that they cannot be taken by armed force. If they can be taken by force, one need not consider the supplies.

XVII. The enemy should be surrounded by camps to prevent any supplies from being brought in or taken out. No one should be allowed to leave, so that it is harder to get supplies. When a city or fortress cannot be surrounded, it must be taken by force. Yet rash attempts at assaults should not be made, and unexpected eruptions by those under siege must be avoided.

XVIII. When besieged, if the city surrenders, one should not hesitate; and the besieger should provide conditions of surrender; the oath of fidelity should be kept sacred, and the agreed conditions fulfilled. If an armed force occupies the city, they should refrain from violence against the defenseless civilians, women, children, and the elderly; only the insurgents should be dealt with harshly. However, the plundering of goods should not be impeded.

XIX. Those fearing siege should fortify their own cities with the work and manpower of the subjects; they should also anticipate victory for a long duration. Those besieged should often attack enemy camps, especially if external reinforcements arrive, which may invade from the rear.

XX. If there is any hope for ending the siege, extreme necessity should not be expected, lest those under siege are compelled to surrender by the besiegers.

XXI. The adjuncts of war include the slaughter of enemies, devastation, demolition, plunder, and pillage. All these are lawful against the enemy as the war itself: but before any treachery is received.

XXII. Captives should be released either for a price or through exchange, according to the quality of the individuals.

XXIII. Criminals, tyrants, deserters, traitors, etc., should not be received into trust; nor, if they have been received through ignorance, should they be kept.

XXIV. The victor commands the defeated, and the defeated must obey the commands; the dominions and all things acquired through war should revert to the Republic unless certain spoils are to be divided among the soldiers.

XXV. It is also useful for security to establish colonies in the subjugated region.

18:

On the Types of War

I. War is variously divided. First, it can be continuous or interrupted by truces. If legitimately concluded, the enemy's faith must be maintained.

II. If after a truce war is re-entered, especially if it has lasted long, it tends to become more bitter and cruel, with forces renewed.

III. If war completely ceases, it is called peace. However, such peace should not be accepted unless it is honorable and secure, or necessary.

IV. If the conditions of peace are tolerable, it should not be rejected. And if it is sanctioned, it should be diligently maintained. The best peace is that which is reached by forgiveness.

V. Secondly, war can be waged either against neighboring nations or distant ones. If it is against distant nations, efforts must be made to ensure that the locals are friendly.

VI. Thirdly, war can be for a proper cause or for a common cause. If a war is undertaken for a common cause, the prince should not abandon his allies; yet he must settle his own affairs, so that if he were to be deserted by others, he could nonetheless manage his own matters well.

VII. Fourthly, there is terrestrial war and naval war: the former is more damaging to the Republic, while the latter is more terrifying for soldiers. However, what pertains specifically to naval warfare significantly concerns naval discipline.

VIII. Fifthly, war can be defensive or offensive. Both are perilous, but offensive war is more so, because we tend to favor those who defend their own rather than those who attack others.

IX. Finally, war can be external or civil, that is, internal. And although all wars are lamentable and to be avoided as much as possible, the most lamentable of all is civil war; for in this, nothing is more miserable than that the very victory leads either to the destruction of the Republic or to its transformation.

X. The prince, aware of the dangers of civil war, should assign to other regions those nobles he suspects, in a manner of honor, and should do all he can to eliminate the causes of civil turmoil.

Chapter 19:

On the Vices of Rule and Causes of Change

I. Just as living bodies have their own diseases and eventually perish, so also political bodies, or Republics, suffer from vices and undergo changes, and finally, they may completely perish.

II. Vices are milder when a prince, either due to long absence or due to a weakening of his mental powers, is deemed less capable of managing affairs. Thus it occurs that he incurs the hatred or contempt of all his subjects.

III. Among the vices of rule and causes of change, the spontaneous abdication of a prince, or death, without a legitimate successor, or an adult heir, is to be counted.

IV. Moreover, the following greatly incite the indignation of subjects and lead them to strive for new things: the intemperance, luxury, indulgence, cruelty, and greed of the prince.

V. These are internal causes; external causes can include migration of peoples, who, having abandoned their homeland due to poverty, seek new places for themselves; or subjugation. The Republic perishes when it is subjected to the power of a foreign prince, as the Romans established many Republics.

VI. A Republic, or principality, degenerates either into anarchy, or into polyarchy, or into tyranny.

VII. Anarchy exists where, without a magistrate, everyone lives according to their own will.

VIII. Polyarchy exists when two or more govern themselves as supreme princes.

IX. Tyranny exists when someone disregards laws, does not regard subjects as citizens, but as slaves.

X. A tyrant either possesses the title of prince or does not.

XI. A tyrant is said to have the title if he is legitimately constituted, although not legitimately ruling.

XII. A tyrant without a title is one who invades the Republic, entrusted neither with succession nor with the right of election, whether by force or deceit.

XIII. Signs of future tyrants can be recognized from many, but a few are notable:

1. If fundamental laws and the privileges of subjects are violated.

2. If he abuses the right of majesty for cruelty or plunder.

3. If he scorns religion, piety, and justice.

4. If he converts public goods and revenues to private uses against the will of the people.

5. If he wishes subjects to live in poverty, or if he fosters divisions among them.

XIV. Whether it is permissible for subjects to kill a tyrant is often debated in politics. This question seems to be resolvable in this way: if anyone acts tyrannically without a title, he may undoubtedly be removed, since he is akin to an enemy.

XV. However, if faith has been pledged to him by a consenting people, he is considered to have a right. And with such a tyrant, another course of action should be taken. If someone has been legitimately constituted as prince, he should not be regarded as a tyrant until he has been declared to have lost his principality by the ephors or nobles of the kingdom, who are meant to protect the rights and privileges of the people.

XVI. It should not be declared that he has lost his principality until manifest signs of tyranny have emerged.

XVII. When he has been duly declared as a tyrant and for violating the faith, having lost his principality, he should be regarded as an enemy, and the people are released from their oath of loyalty.

Chapter 20:

On Religion

I. Just as a person cannot be happy without religion, neither can a political body be blessed if religion is despised.

II. Nor should religion be a pretext or an excuse for the prince to keep subjects in line; rather, he must genuinely care for it and set an example for his subjects.

III. To this end, the prince claims a certain right of majesty over the Church. This includes:

The right to summon and appoint ministers of the churches within his jurisdiction.

The right to sanction and promulgate laws regarding ecclesiastical order and discipline, as well as ecclesiastical judgments.

IV. However, he should establish nothing in these matters without first consulting ecclesiastical councils. It is also useful for the prince to have men of faith among his advisors, experts in discipline and ecclesiastical law, whose counsel he may use in matters pertaining to the Church.

V. The prince should restrain blasphemers and perjurers, as well as impostors and seducers, who not only err in their thoughts about God and religion, but also seek to lead others astray and maliciously disturb the peace of the Church.

VI. Furthermore, the prince should protect the Church against external harm and injury. He should also establish revenues for it, preserve those revenues, and ensure that honest wages are paid to ecclesiastical officials. He should not easily allow goods designated for the Church to be diverted to profane uses.

VII. And because there is no greater good in the Republic than consensus in religion, the prince should strive by all means to prevent dissensions from arising, before conflicts heat up and rumors spread.

VIII. To this end, he should convene synods or ecclesiastical assemblies, in which controversies should be known and judgments passed, in which he himself, either personally or by his delegates, presides.

IX. If anyone deviates from the true religion, they should not be punished with exiles or punishments, except when something politically reprehensible has occurred. For the prince should not claim authority over consciences. Faith must be offered freely, not coerced.

And diversity of religions among subjects does not destroy the unity of the polity.

X. If any agreements or safe conduct have been granted to dissenting subjects regarding religion, the prince must uphold them. However, it is deadly to maintain faith with heretics.

XI. These matters pertain to the prince: the duty of the subjects regarding religion is to recognize the prince's right and majesty in ecclesiastical matters and to obey him in all things that he commands regarding the word of God, worship, and religion.

XII. Nor should ecclesiastical persons be allowed to appeal to foreign jurisdiction. For since they are part of the Republic (unless someone wishes to establish the Republic in a manner contrary to this), they should also submit to the political magistrate like all other members.

XIII. If the prince is alienated from true religion, he does not thereby cease to be a legitimate prince; much less should he be regarded as a tyrant on that account.

XIV. Thus, subjects should not rise up against the prince on account of religion, provided he does not inflict persecutions. If such should occur, private citizens should seek to escape persecution or endure it until the nobles or the lower magistrates can defend and protect them.

21:

On the Points of Commonality Between Aristocracy and Democracy

I. Thus far, all these things have been said concerning Monarchy or Principality, which must also be appropriately adapted to Aristocracy and Democracy in a certain way.

II. Besides a few remaining observations, which are either common to both Aristocracy and Democracy or particular to each, we will first discuss the common aspects of both.

III. The monarchical status is undoubtedly the best by its nature, as it is not subject to discord; and a state in which the empire is under the authority of many is commendable to the extent that it is reduced to unity. This unity consists of consensus and concord.

IV. Since the governance and exercise of jurisdiction are not concentrated in one solid person, it is agreed that someone should be elected through common suffrage, who, as a minister, exercises jurisdiction; or those who rule may exercise jurisdiction in turn.

V. Where there is distrust in voting, decrees must be established from multiple votes; otherwise, the state can easily be disturbed.

VI. In extremely perilous matters, it is useful for the supreme authority of the Republic to be entrusted to one or another, who should provide extraordinary counsel to ensure that nothing harms the Republic.

VII. Those who govern in a state of many should be divided into orders: senators, executors, and judges.

VIII. In time of war, a commander or general should be created, who has supreme military authority, since such councils are not suitable for warfare.

22:

On Aristocracy

I. Aristocracy is a state in which a few excellent individuals are granted the right of majesty and command over the rest.

II. Because fewer govern in Aristocracy than in Democracy, it is also a more perfect state, approaching unity.

III. The right to command belongs to the nobility collectively and equally to all.

IV. The right to summon colleagues, propose matters for deliberation, request and gather votes, must be transferred to one, who may serve in that role either permanently or temporarily.

V. They should keep their counsels secret, and anyone who reveals what should be kept silent should be removed from command.

VI. The nobles may be elected either by themselves (which should scarcely occur unless in the establishment of an Aristocratic empire) or by the votes of the other nobles. This is much safer than allowing the power to elect nobles to the people.

VII. When choosing individuals, prudence and virtue should be especially regarded; additionally, nobility, wealth, age, and so forth.

VIII. However, the nobles either have supreme authority, like the Venetians, and this is the true Aristocracy; or they acknowledge someone superior in the land, as occurs in many cities of Germany.

IX. Furthermore, the authority of the nobility is either perpetual or temporary.

X. The disease of this state is the discord of the nobility, which, unless timely restrained, leads to Oligarchy, which is like the downfall of Aristocracy.

XI. Oligarchy occurs when a few among the nobles, excluding their colleagues, seize power and, disregarding the laws, oppress the remaining multitude.

XII. This must be feared by the nobles themselves. They must also fear that subjects might want to change Aristocracy into Democracy, which the multitude and the common people largely depend on.

XIII. To prevent this, the nobles must ensure that the common people are not incited against the nobility and should severely punish those who are found to have attempted such a thing.

23:

On Democracy

I. Democracy is a state in which, either in the name of all citizens or of a large part, some rule over others universally and exercise the right of majesty and supreme power.

II. Democracy is the most imperfect state by its nature, as it strays farthest from unity. Nevertheless, due to particular circumstances, it is often to be preferred over the others.

III. In this state, the right of majesty belongs to the entire populace, whose authority is exercised by appointed magistrates.

IV. To streamline the gathering of votes from individuals, prefects of tribes or certain classes are established, who will carry votes for their tribes or classes in appointing magistrates.

V. Thus, the nature of Democracy is rooted in the equality of honors, rights, and liberties; so that one person does not wish to obey another, unless that person exercises authority over those whom they have obeyed.

VI. To prevent this equality from being hindered by the authority of illustrious and prominent individuals, they should be ostracized, as Athenians did, or exiled, as the Spartans did.

VII. It is useful in a Democracy to prohibit reckless accusations, as well as the confiscation of the goods of the good, lest the authority of the populace diminish and resources be exhausted, leading to Oligarchy, Anarchy, or to Monarchy, Aristocracy, or Timocracy, which is a state in which the wealthy rule, excluding the poorer citizens.

VIII. Such inconveniences or vices should be avoided. The authority of magistrates should be restrained to prevent overreach.

IX. In contrast, the magistrates should study the public good more than the favor of the populace. They should restrain those who seek to win the people over through flattery and burden the wealthy with calumnies, thus introducing resentment and envy.

24:

On Mixed Forms of Government

I. Thus far, we have dealt with simple forms of the Republic; now follow mixed forms. A Republic is mixed either from Monarchy and Aristocracy, or from Aristocracy and Democracy, or from Monarchy, Aristocracy, and Democracy.

II. The mixed status of Monarchy and Aristocracy seems to be the most eminent of all. For it possesses the advantages of both, along with remedies against the evils that threaten from either.

III. Monarchy in this state must have supreme power. Therefore, it should not achieve anything significant, or be able to, without the consent of the nobles.

IV. Certain agreements should intercede between the prince and the nobles, by which they bind themselves to the Republic and to one another. These agreements are the foundations of this state.

V. The prince should be elected from among the nobles and from the nobles. This should be done rather by secret calculations than by open votes or suffrages.

VI. The nobles should also be chosen by the prince and by the nobles, not from the plebeians but from the sons of the nobles.

VII. Once elected, the prince should swear to the nobles that he will ensure nothing harms the Republic and will maintain all agreements and fundamental laws. Similarly, those elected from the body of nobles will swear to the prince.

VIII. Therefore, the prince is superior to all the nobles; when all are together, he is inferior. Thus, as nothing can exist without a mutual relationship, the popular magistrate must be elected from the whole body by votes, who commands for a time, alongside the Senatorial order, and primarily ensures that the common people are not burdened with unfair tributes or other burdens.

IX. However, sometimes Aristocracy predominates, sometimes Democracy. Where Aristocracy predominates, magistrates should be elected from primary citizens: they must carefully safeguard their rights so that these are not taken away from them by the common people.

X. If the common people have their own assemblies and trades unions, their leaders should be the nobles, and from those assemblies, someone should participate from the nobility.

XI. Where Democracy prevails, everything is conducted in the opposite way: artisans are also elected to the Senate, and they have their own assemblies even in the presence of the nobles, whose leaders they constitute.

XII. When this state becomes corrupted or distorted, it will end either in Oligarchy or in Ochlocracy: the former brings the downfall of the nobles, the latter that of the common people.

XIII. Finally, there is a state tempered from Monarchy, Aristocracy, and Democracy. This state seems to be the most protective of all, as it prevents the other two forms from being able to disturb the Republic. It often arises when subjects suffer under Monarchy or Aristocracy.

XIV. This state is suitable for cities that have extensive dominions or whole provinces. For in a narrow dominion, the splendor of Monarchy cannot have a place.

XV. It is difficult for this state to be equally tempered from the three forms. However, it often happens that one or two dominate while the others are merely present. Sometimes Monarchy predominates, sometimes Aristocracy, and sometimes Democracy, with the other forms.

XVI. Where Monarchy predominates, no assemblies should be granted to the nobles or the common people unless the Monarch presides over them.

XVII. Where Aristocracy prevails, it is necessary for the nobles to have their own gatherings; they cannot write letters in the name of the Republic to outsiders unless they have the right to summon the nobles, propose matters for consultation, and request votes.

XVIII. If the prince commits an offense, it is the duty of the nobles to admonish him, to correct him, to reprimand him, to punish him, or even to condemn him. If they neglect this, the blame for the mismanagement of the Republic must be attributed even to the nobles, which is extremely disgraceful for them, to flatter the prince to the extent that they only act at his behest.

XIX. Furthermore, in this state, either Monarchy or Aristocracy predominates. Monarchy prevails when the prince has greater authority than the nobles. When this occurs, succession may take place. However, it cannot happen where Aristocracy prevails.

XX. The state derived from Aristocracy and Democracy is said to exist when the nobility rule in such a way that the people also participate in governance.

XXI. Therefore, in this state, there should be a dual magistracy, and dual suffrage, of nobles and of the people. The people, along with the nobles, should rule through delegates, who act in place of the people for a time. Such positions in the Roman Republic were called Tribunes of the Plebs.

XXII. This state is suitable for governing individual cities, especially those where commerce and crafts thrive; for in Monarchy, the excessive power of nobles and courtly individuals is burdensome for merchants and craftsmen. In the governance of individual cities, apart from the laws of nature and of nations, a municipal law exists, or specific statutes for individual cities.

XXIII. The governance should thus be instituted in such a way that it is divided into three orders: the senatorial order, the judges, and the popular order.

XXIV. The number of Senators cannot be precisely defined, nor can the variety of ranks; all of which depend on the diverse constitutions of cities.

XXV. Nevertheless, among all, one should be designated to indicate the assembly, preside there, propose matters for deliberation, request votes, gather them, receive petitions, sign letters, safeguard the seal, and so forth. This also applies to the order of judges.

XXVI. The people are considered as magistrates, or as subjects. They may convene to deliberate about defending their prerogatives.

XXVII. A state in which the populace predominates in a mixed manner over Monarchy or Aristocracy is not easily established, nor can it be relied upon, as it could be enduring.

XXVIII. Thus, it is said that Democracy predominates when a prominent part of the populace, superior in lineage and wealth, predominates over the Monarch and the Nobles.

XXIX. Where Monarchy prevails with Aristocracy, care must be taken not to completely exclude the people from governance. Thus, in other forms, the third order should strive to safeguard its own power, so that it is not completely excluded by the other two orders, which predominate.

Other books currently available from Sacra Press:

A Treatise of Christian Religion
by Thomas Cartwright
Father of the Puritans & of Presbyterianism displays the full jewels of a systematic theology in a catechetical format. Newly republished for the first time in centuries.

The Old Faith
by Henry Bullinger
Titanic Swiss Reformer weaves a mixed work of biblical & covenant theology, born of pastoral concerns, to prove the antiquity of the Christian Faith.

Lectures On Human Nature
by Samuel Doak
18th century American Presbyterian, church-planter, and school teacher keenly pens an introductory philosophy of human nature. Includes his sermon to the Overmountain Men just before their victory at King's Mountain.

A Precept for the Baptism of Infants
by Nathaniel Stephens
17th century non-conformist Minister proves the precept of paedobaptism from the New Testament in response to the objection of anti-paedobaptists.

The Cambridge & Saybrook Platforms
by Miscellaneous Ministers
New England Congregationalists inscribe their polity.

Books soon-to-be or now published by Sacra Press:

On the First Sin of Adam
by Franciscus Junius
French Protestant Reformer and theologian explores Adam's first sin and its relation to God's foreknowledge and decree, necessity, and free will.

On the Establishment of the Republic
by Francesco Patrizi
Roman Catholic bishop and key Renaissance philosopher of the 15th century marshals myriad classical sources to construct a treatise of virtue-politics.

The Christian Obligations of Citizenship
by John G. Sheppard
19th century Anglican academic exploits logic, rhetoric, history, classical sources, and Scripture to construct his Christian political theory.

Positive Christianity in the Third Reich
by Cajus Fabricius
Protestant Theologian and NSDAP party member writes to show the compatibility between National Socialism and a certain form of Christianity. Includes The 28 Theses of the German Christians.

With many more to come—Lord willing.

Visit www.sacrapress.com/armory to purchase available books, to stay updated on releases, and more.

www.ingramcontent.com/pod-product-compliance
Lightning Source LLC
Chambersburg PA
CBHW022056020426
42335CB00012B/706